D1611946

THE DESTINY
OF GOLD

THE DESTINY
OF GOLD

PAUL EINZIG

MACMILLAN
ST MARTIN'S PRESS

First published 1972 by
THE MACMILLAN PRESS LTD
London and Basingstoke
Associated companies in New York Toronto
Dublin Melbourne Johannesburg and Madras

Library of Congress catalog card no. 72-85830

SBN 333 14291 8

Printed in Great Britain by
R. & R. CLARK LTD
Edinburgh

Contents

Preface

THIS is my fourth book dealing with the monetary role of gold, written following on a long interval after the first three – *International Gold Movements* (1929), *The Future of Gold* (1935) and *Will Gold Depreciate?* (1937). It is a subject to which I have always attached considerable importance, and the fact that it is now distinctly out of fashion to favour the retention of gold's monetary role does not make any difference to my attitude. Anyhow, it has been my experience that, if only one adheres to an unfashionable view long enough, sooner or later it becomes fashionable once more.

This book's main claim for originality lies in my contention that gold is indispensable in the monetary system because of environmental considerations. The relative scarcity of gold and the resulting inadequacy of its monetary supply in face of an insatiable demand acted as nature's balance that tended to mitigate the debasement of the environment.

It is most unfortunate, indeed a tragedy, that the monetary role of gold has been greatly weakened just when it has become much more important than ever, owing to the application of permissiveness to the monetary system, that nature's balancing function should mitigate the debasement of the environment brought about by the inflationary misuse of money.

The fact that the monetary aspect of environment protection was not touched in the recently published report on *The Limits of Growth* by the Club of Rome – a Committee investigating problems of the environment on which economists were strongly represented – indicates the need for drawing attention to this aspect of the subject. It introduces a new element into the controversy over the monetary role of gold, controversy in which the antagonists have argued each other more or less to a standstill.

The Destiny of Gold follows closely on my book *The Destiny of the Dollar*. In some respects the two books deal with two aspects of the same subject, for the case for and against a higher price of gold is largely, though not entirely, identical with the case for and against a major devaluation of the dollar. But the case for and against a de-monetisation of gold is a different though related problem. Although it is also discussed in my book on the dollar, it is the central theme of the present book. And even the price of gold is discussed from a different angle. The impact of the monetary aspects of gold on environmental problems is barely mentioned in *The Destiny of the Dollar*. It was because I came to realise the overwhelming importance of the destructive effects of inflation on the environment that I decided to write the present book.

Crusaders in favour of de-monetising gold and opponents of raising its official price include expansionist economists swimming with the tide, and politicians wanting to remove any interference with their bid for popularity through pursuing inflationary policies regardless of their destructive effects on the environment. The camp includes bankers and businessmen who are anxious to avoid being handicapped by credit restraint. That attitude is so prevalent in financial circles that some years ago I even had to defend the case for gold on the premises of a Central Bank which has always been looked upon as the shrine of the cult of the golden calf. And I had to speak on one occasion for the *raison d'être* of gold in the very room where its London market price is fixed twice a day, arguing against the de-monetisation of gold while beholding ashtrays full of cigarette butts deposited only a few minutes earlier in the course of the fixing.

Having regard to the above, I feel that no apology is called for producing a book that states the argument for retaining the monetary role of gold. It is intended as an eleventh-hour appeal against the decision made by several Governments – including those of the United States and Britain – to ease gold out of the monetary system.

P. E.

120 Clifford's Inn
London E.C.4
April 1972

CHAPTER ONE

Why Gold?

THE most stable period in international monetary history was the century between the Napoleonic Wars and the First World War. No doubt *Pax Britannica* had had a great deal to do with the relative absence of universal currency chaos, such as had occurred in previous centuries and again during the decades that followed the outbreak of the First World War. But the increasing monetary role played by gold during the nineteenth century also went a long way towards mitigating disturbing monetary fluctuations. It is no sheer coincidence that during the last quarter of the nineteenth century and the years up to 1914, when the gold standard replaced gradually the silver standard, the bimetallist system and the inconvertible paper currencies in many advanced countries, the number and extent of monetary upheavals was less than in any other comparable period of monetary history.

No wonder some of us still firmly hold the view that if gold had not existed as the basis of monetary system, it ought to have been invented. That view has become unpopular in recent years not only among economists and politicians but also among many bankers, including Central Bankers. The prevailing fashion is at the time of writing to preach the de-monetisation of gold – the gradual reduction of what is left of its monetary role. It is considered to be hopelessly out of date positively to adhere to the view that gold must play an essential part in the international monetary system and that its elimination would be gravely disadvantageous from the point of view of the world's monetary and economic stability.

The origin of the monetary role of gold can be traced back

to Antiquity. During many early centuries gold changing hands by weight was an important medium of exchange, standard of value and store of wealth, even though during most of the time it shared this role with other metals, primarily with silver. The importance of the monetary role of gold increased considerably with the adoption of coinage, especially after certain coins came to command sufficient confidence to change hand by tale instead of changing hands by weight. During the late Ancient Period gold coins shared their monetary role with silver coins on a more or less equal footing. But in medieval times the inadequacy of gold output reduced the monetary role of gold to second place after silver coins.

Following on the discovery of America gold came into its own as a result of the increase of its supply. Even though silver was used more actively in internal traffic – most people could not afford to use gold coins – gold was found more suitable for international transactions, owing to its relatively high value which reduced the cost of its transport across the sea and across land frontiers.

Silver retained its role as the more widely used currency right until the nineteenth century. It was not until after the Napoleonic Wars that Britain adopted the gold standard and her example was followed only very gradually by other countries. Until the last three decades of the nineteenth century a number of advanced countries used the two metals jointly under the system of bimetallism, or they used inconvertible paper currency stabilised in terms of gold or silver. Less advanced countries employed silver as their principal monetary metal right until after the First World War.

The gold standard, under which gold coins and notes convertible into gold were legal tender and free international gold movements kept exchange rates stable within their gold export points and gold import points came to be adopted in an increasing number of countries which were able to maintain the necessary sound financial conditions. Admittedly the number of countries on a really effective gold standard was very small even during the years immediately before 1914. Many more countries endeavoured to maintain their exchanges stable in terms of currencies on the gold standard without adopting free convertibility of their notes into gold. Several leading countries, while nominally on the gold standard, resorted to various devices to discourage the outflow of gold and to stimulate artificially its inflow. But disregarding such technicalities it was broadly correct to say that most advanced countries had monetary systems based on gold.

Gold coins were in circulation in a number of countries side by side with notes which came to assume monetary role during the eighteenth century and even more during the nineteenth century. These bank notes or State paper moneys owed their stability mainly to their convertibility into gold – or to the hope that they would become convertible. The awareness that they could be used in payments of every kind because recipients in turn were able to use them in payment and because the State authority made its acceptance compulsory emerged only gradually. Even in countries where the notes were not actually convertible either into gold coins or into silver coins they were regarded as substitutes for coins and their value depended largely on the prospects of their convertibility, but also on their relative scarcity due to the limitation of their supply.

While in Latin America and in some of the less stable countries in Europe the fall of the external value of inconvertible currencies was accompanied by the fall of their domestic purchasing power, most European inconvertible currencies – such as the Austro-Hungarian krone and the Russian rouble – were stable during the years preceeding the First World War in spite of being inconvertible. The domestic price level in such countries was very roughly in equilibrium with the price levels in countries which were on an effective gold standard.

It should not be assumed, however, that the extensive and increasing monetary use of gold had created a carefree state of affairs, even though it seemed so to subsequent generations when viewing pre-1914 conditions in retrospect. Although the foreign exchange 'crises' of that period came to be looked upon subsequently as having been insignificant, it did not seem so to the contemporary generations. And the stability of the monetary system based largely on gold did not prevent cyclic economic crises aggravated by speculative booms and disastrous slumps.

The system came under much criticism on the ground that monetary stability had been maintained at the cost of keeping down economic growth. Considering the remarkable progress achieved during the nineteenth century, such criticism was surely grossly exaggerated. Nevertheless in many quarters it greatly mitigated the popularity of the system because under it economic expansion had been handicapped by the need for maintaining the currencies stable in terms of gold.

Nor had been prices as stable as they appear in retrospect. Although in the course of any one year price movements were narrow, basic price trends had been in operation and had been largely determined by changes in the output of gold resulting from discoveries or absence of discoveries of new goldfields. The progressive de-monetisation of silver was also an important factor during the last three decades of the century.

Even allowing for all this, the pre-1914 gold standard had been an incomparably more stable system than either the monetary systems that had been in operation in earlier periods or those that had been in operation in more recent times. Earlier forms of metallic currencies suffered from debasements on the one hand and from chronic inadequacy of the supply of coins in circulation on the other. The invention of paper money in Europe provided opportunities for violent inflations such as those witnesses in France as a result of the experiment of John Law and even more during the French Revolution, or in Russia and Austria over prolonged periods, or in the United States during the Civil War. Instability of exchanges due to the changing relationship between the value of gold and silver gradually disappeared as and when more and more countries adhered to gold.

The extent to which stability had to be achieved under the gold standard, and under stable monetary systems in general, at the cost of slowing down progress is grossly exaggerated in our days by those suffering from growth-hysteria. The restrictive effect of stability had not prevented the financing of the Industrial Revolution in Europe and in the United States, the exploitation of technological inventions, the construction of a costly transport system and the slow but by no means insignificant increase of the standard of living.

The main advantage of the monetary use of gold was that it had tidied up the monetary system and had introduced order where chaos prevailed prior to the increasing adoption of the various degrees and forms of gold standard. Its achievement and maintenance imposed a high degree of discipline on the economies of the countries that had adopted it or had aimed at adopting it. They had to make a serious effort to keep their Budgets and their balances of payments reasonably balanced, for deficits in either sphere were liable to endanger the achievement or maintenance of the gold standard. Unsound policies carried their own penalties in the form of a depreciation of the exchanges and the automatic reduction of gold or foreign exchange reserves. They also carried their automatic correctives, since a decline in the gold reserve entailed a contraction of the supply of currency and credit which tended to improve the balance of payments.

Admittedly the development of an extensive system of international lending and investment made it possible for overspending countries to have Budgetary deficits and balance of payments deficits over long periods, provided that they were able to borrow abroad and were prepared to pay the relatively high costs of borrowing from naturally distrustful foreign investors. But the borrowing capacity of capital-importing countries was not unlimited, and there was an incentive for them to maintain or restore sound or relatively sound conditions, in order to be creditworthy. Movements of short-term funds and international short-term borrowing or lending filled temporary gaps, but it did not do away with the necessity for aiming at the enforcement of a certain degree of Budgetary or balance of payments discipline.

On the eve of the First World War gold appeared to be firmly established as the basis of the world's monetary system. It looked probable that more and more countries would adhere to the system under which exchange movements were fractional and tended to carry their own automatic correctives. The advantages of the use of gold as the reserves of countries enabling them to meet deficits on their balance of payments came to be generally realised. Exporting countries were not always in a position to find buyers abroad for all their exportable surpluses, importing countries were not always able to pay for all that they wanted to import. The possession of adequate gold reserves provided the answer for both problems. Gold was accepted in payment for import surpluses in unlimited amounts, and countries unable to sell abroad goods and services of sufficient value to meet their requirements were able to fall back on their gold holdings. Possession of gold reserves above immediate requirements inspired confidence abroad and made it possible to expand at home without endangering the external stability of the national currency.

It was substantially correct to say that the period of the pre-1914 gold standard had been (in more than one sense) the golden age of mankind. It is true, the gold standard may have slowed down the increase in the standard of living. But the contention that under the gold standard economic growth and prosperity were at the mercy of the caprices of nature was grossly exaggerated. Admittedly, the increase in the volume of newly mined monetary gold did not always keep pace with the increase in monetary requirements. But the existence of sound gold foundations for the monetary system had inspired confidence enabling the advanced countries to develop an extensive credit system, which would have been impossible without the confidence-inspiring effect of the possession of monetary gold that could be relied upon for being always in demand and which was therefore always accepted. Had it not been for the sound foundations of the monetary system the development of the credit system would have been much slower, and setbacks in its expansion would have been both more frequent and more violent. The fact that the volume of credit continued to expand after the Second World War even though the proportion of the world's monetary gold to the total volume of money declined to a fraction of its pre-1914 figure does not prove that a confidence-inspiring volume of monetary gold would not have been advantageous at earlier phases of the evolution of the national and international credit system.

It was largely thanks to the existence of substantial amounts of monetary gold that a strong banking system was able to develop, for the great benefit of production, commerce and consumption. There was a long way to progress from the primitive banking system operating in earlier centuries to the relatively sophisticated and advanced banking system of the late nineteenth century and early twentieth century. And the progress that made it possible for banks to inspire the required degree of confidence was largely the result of the existence of substantial monetary gold reserves. Had banks attempted a hundred years earlier to build up a super-pyramid of uncovered non-self liquidating credits comparable in magnitude to those which exist in our days it is certain that the result would have been disastrous crises causing sharp setbacks in economic progress and inflicting grave hardships on mankind.

In the nineteenth century it was absolutely essential to base the credit structure on money with intrinsic value. Even if those who contend that today such money is no longer necessary were right they are absolutely wrong in denying that gold had played a historical role in creating the degree of confidence necessary for building up an extensive credit structure. The beneficial effects of possessing a metallic currency the scarcity-value and intrinsic value of which had enabled it to inspire absolute confidence and to ensure a perpetual excess of demand over its supply had been incalculable.

The choice of gold as the basis of the monetary system had not been the result of any international agreement comparable with the Bretton Woods Agreement leading to the establishment of the International Monetary Fund, or with the Rio de Janeiro Agreement providing for the issue of Special Drawing

Rights. Mankind had stumbled on the right solution through trial and error. Country after country drifted towards the adoption of gold as the basis for its currency as and when it had been able to afford to do so and had the required degree of willpower and self-restraint to enable it to maintain sound finances and to acquire and maintain, as a result, the necessary amount of gold. On the face of it it might appear that, had it not been for the policies adopted in order to build up substantial gold reserves, the countries concerned might have been able to produce or import more consumer goods and their population would have had a better time. Likewise, the maintenance of a sufficiently large gold reserve to ensure the satisfactory operation of the gold standard called for policies aimed at ensuring some degree of self-restraint. Had it not been for the automatic effect of gold outflows on the volume of credit, and through it on production and consumption, a higher degree of temporary prosperity might have been achieved. But the prosperity thus created would have been built on much less dependable foundations. For the sake of having a good time future progress depending on the achievement and maintenance of a lasting solid monetary and credit system would have been sacrificed.

It came to be realised during the late nineteenth century and the early twentieth century that the possession of substantial gold reserves, or of claims that were convertible into gold – such as British acceptance credits – represented power and prestige. Even in earlier centuries it was largely thanks to her monetary power that Britain was able to play a decisive role in world history, using her ability to secure the support of allies and to finance prolonged wars enabling her to win the last battle. By the end of the nineteenth century financial power came to assume the form of possessing or being able to acquire large amounts of gold and of a credits system that inspired confidence based on the possession of gold and on capacity to acquire it.

CHAPTER TWO

A Symbol of Stability

ONE of the main reasons why the monetary role of gold is still favoured in many quarters is because it is considered a symbol of monetary and economic stability. The monetary system must surely have a 'fixed point' which can be depended upon in this world of uncertainties. It has been a long-established opinion that money cannot perform its function adequately unless it is stable. This quality is advantageous if a currency is to serve as a medium of exchange, though a moderate degree of instability does not prevent it from being used in payment for goods and services. Its stability is more important for its function as a standard of value, because a measuring rod which keeps changing its length would have distinct disadvantages. It is equally important that a store of wealth and a standard of deferred payments should have a stable value, so that it could be depended upon by debtors and creditors alike.

From this point of view gold is highly suitable for fulfilling its monetary task. Admittedly it is not the only conceivable stable standard of deferred payments or store of wealth. There are many instances of the use of unstable currencies for those purposes, with the application of some formula by which the nominal amount of the claim or the liability in terms of current monetary units is adjusted according to changes in the value of gold or in the average price level or in the cost of living, in terms of the current monetary unit. Or the lender may have the option to choose the currency in which interest and principal are payable. All these formulas have their disadvantages and they certainly have their complications. They are not nearly as simple and straightforward as the formula under which a claim is receivable or a liability is payable in terms of the current monetary unit the value of which is, in turn, fixed in terms of a certain weight of gold.

Admittedly, as experience has amply proved, the gold value of monetary units is not fixed permanently. It is subject to adjustment by legislative measures. The gold parity of sterling was reduced on two occasions since the war. A currency may be devalued or revalued, in which case the gold equivalent of the claims or liabilities fixed in terms of that currency is changed accordingly. But under a stable monetary system such changes are few and far between. During the interval between such changes of parities the currencies are stable in terms of gold. Which does not mean that their value is stable in terms of purchasing power, for, as we shall see in Chapter 12, the purchasing power of gold itself in terms of goods and services is subject to changes. Nevertheless, gold has long been considered a symbol of stability. A currency that is stable in terms of gold is considered to be more stable than a currency the value of which would be fixed in terms of any other single commodity. It is arguable that it is not so stable as a money the value of which is adjusted according to changes in average prices of a number of commodities. But mankind had so far very little experience in such system and the maintenance of the value of a currency in terms of gold is widely regarded as the most stable system in practice.

Possibly a time might come when stability would mean stability in terms of goods. During the 'twenties the gold standard was criticised a great deal on the ground that it did not assure for the monetary unit sufficient stability in terms of commodities. Professor Irving Fisher among others suggested that the monetary unit in terms of which the goods are bought and sold and in terms of which liabilities are incurred or settled should be fixed in terms of a 'goods basket' – a composite unit of account in which goods are represented according to their relative importance. But nothing had come of this proposal and during the period of relative stability in the 'twenties gold was generally regarded as the ideal standard of value – or at any rate as being as near the ideal as we could expect it to be in this imperfect world of ours.

When a currency is stabilised it means that its international value is fixed in terms of gold. When it is maintained stable it means that its value is kept unchanged in terms of gold. When a system of floating currencies is adopted it means that the value of the monetary unit is allowed to fluctuate in terms of other currencies and also in terms of gold. When in 1946 the parities of currencies were fixed in terms of gold as well as of dollars under the rules of the IMF this was because, since the dollar was convertible into gold – at any rate for official holders – the fixing of parities in terms of dollars was considered to be just another way of expressing their value in terms of a fixed quantity of gold.

Those who are in favour of monetary flexibility are opposed to the maintenance of fixed gold parities. So long as the value of a currency is fixed in terms of a certain quantity of gold it remains more or less stable in terms of all other currencies the parities of which are also expressed in terms of a certain quantity of gold. Stability in terms of gold does not of course prevent the fluctuation of the currencies in terms of commodities, because gold itself need not necessarily be stable in terms of commodities. But the maintenance of currencies stable in terms of gold is considered to be the highest degree of stability that is practicable under the existing system.

It is true, when there is an upward or downward trend in prices abroad a country would be able to insulate its economy from the world trend by adjusting the value of its currency in terms of other currencies. And if the latter are stable in terms of gold this would mean adjusting its value also in terms of gold. When in September 1931 Britain suspended the gold standard it meant that sterling was allowed to fluctuate in terms of the dollar, the franc and a number of other currencies the value of which was kept stable in terms of gold. As a result the British price level was no longer linked with the price levels of countries with currencies kept stable in terms of gold.

Situations are apt to arise in which there is a choice between keeping a currency stable in terms of gold or in terms of the average prices of goods. It is a matter of opinion which is the real stability. But according to the most widely accepted opinion it is stability in terms of gold that counts as real stability. For one thing it may be open to argument whether stability of a currency in terms of goods means the stability of retail prices or of wholesale prices; whether only international traded goods should be taken into consideration; how the average of the prices of goods should be weighted ; whether the weighting should be permanent or adaptable to changing conditions, and so forth. Stability in terms of gold involves no such complicated considerations.

It is true, there can be more than one gold price. Since the adoption of the two-tier system there is the official price and the market price. Even before the adoption of that system the market price of gold was not internationally uniform, it was much higher in hoarding countries such as India. But the widely accepted rule is that stability of a currency means its stability in terms of the official price of gold. Stability need not mean absolute rigidity. It means the maintenance of the exchange rates in the close vicinity of their gold parities. Exchange rates may be subject to fluctuations around their parities – under the gold standard between their gold import points and their gold export points, under the Bretton Woods system between their maximum and minimum support points. Forward rates are of course subject to much wider fluctuations without limits. But so long as spot rates do not exceed their 'band' around their parities the exchanges are considered stable in spite of any erratic movements within their support prints. So long as the exchange rates are in the vicinity of their gold parities they are stable. A certain fixed weight of gold is supposed to represent their value. Under that system gold is the symbol of monetary stability.

Possibly this state of affairs is not permanent. It might have been changed if the annual output of newly mined gold had come to represent a higher proportion of the existing stock of gold. Or if the amount of hoarded gold had greatly exceeded that of monetary gold stocks, and large-scale de-hoarding or increase in hoarding demand might have unsettled the stability of the value of gold. But in existing circumstances the value of gold is more stable even now than any other metal or any non-metallic material. It is certainly more stable than silver the price of which had considerable ups and downs in recent years. It is much more stable than platinum.

Admittedly the stability of the value of gold is largely the result of its extensive monetary use, so that it is arguable that in a sense the contention that gold is the most suitable monetary material because of its stability is begging the question. But stability is not the only reason for gold's unique prestige since time immemorial. Although platinum is much more valuable, somehow it does not command the same prestige as gold. That prestige is deeply rooted in human nature and cannot be explained altogether on rational grounds. Most people like to possess gold in some form. It is the favourite means by which possessions are hoarded and displayed. Whenever trouble is threatening the inhabitants of countries with hoarding habits increases their gold hoards. Gold coins or gold objects in other form are preferred to some even more valuable and more easily concealable objects, presumably because gold is more easily marketable owing to the uniformity of its quality.

So long as this preference of hoarders for gold continues – and there is no reason to suppose that it will not continue indefinitely subject to temporary ups and downs of its extent – it goes a long way towards ensuring the maintenance of the privileged position of gold. Balance of payments surpluses, in so far as they do not find their way into official reserves, are liable to be mopped up by hoarders. Hoarding is not necessarily a stabilising influence, however. Any considerable increase of its extent, or any considerable de-hoarding, is liable to affect the value of gold. Its market price is liable to be unsettled also by speculation anticipating changes in its official or unofficial price. Even allowing for all this, however, gold is likely to continue to symbolise monetary stability.

Gold as a commodity is not a necessity, and its possession does not directly satisfy any essential human needs. But non-monetary demand is no passing fashion, having been in evidence since the earliest recorded days of civilisation. It is due in part to its relative scarcity, but also to its decorative quality. Even though in our generation it has disappeared from monetary circulation, there are few people who would not possess gold coins or other objects of gold if they can afford to acquire it. I myself have known several very vocal opponents of the monetary role of gold who possessed gold watches, cigarette cases or other objects, even though stainless steel or other metals would have served their practical purposes perfectly well. This preference for gold seems to be a well-established taste which is not subject to the fluctuation of fashion. It goes some way towards ensuring for gold a permanent place in the monetary system.

CHAPTER THREE

Campaigns Against Gold

THE predominant monetary role of gold was not maintained without opposition, that was encountered during various phases of monetary history. Attacks on that role which are experienced in our days had many precedents. This is not the first time that the elimination of gold – or of precious metals in general – from the monetary system is urged or attempted. The first historical precedent was created in Sparta by Lycurgus (*c.* 825 B.C.) according to Plutarch. He introduced a monetary system under which the State authority made it compulsory to employ as media of exchange iron bars rendered useless for practical purposes by a special process. The possession of coins or precious metals was outlawed and was subject to severe penalties. Only the Government itself was permitted to own coins which were used exclusively for the requirements of foreign trade or other payments abroad. This experiment to do away with money that possessed intrinsic metallic value had failed, however, judging by the fact that hoards of foreign coins were frequently discovered in Sparta, especially after Lysander secured rich war booties as a result of his victories.

A similar system was advocated several centuries later by Plato, but he made no reference to the failure of the attempt made in Sparta to adopt it, or indeed to the fact that such an attempt had been made before his time.

Another well-known historical experiment, much nearer our time, was that of John Law in France during the early part of the eighteenth century. It coincided more or less with the South Sea Bubble in England and with the frenzied speculation in tulip bulbs in the Netherlands. John Law persuaded the

Regent's Government – like Mephistopheles persuaded the Emperor in *Faust*, Part II – to authorise the issue of paper money. In order to increase confidence in the currency of his invention, Law caused the official price of gold coins to be changed frequently in the naïve hope of conveying the impression that the value of the coins was unstable and that therefore they were undependable. So long as the quantity of paper money was kept relatively moderate all was well. But there was too much temptation and too much opportunity to abuse the system by over-issuing the paper money. The disastrous outcome of the John Law experience is a matter of general knowledge. Nor does his subsequent apologia, blaming the Government for the misuse of his paper currency, carry any conviction. After all, it was the application of his system that had removed discipline from the French monetary system, providing temptation and opportunity for an irresponsible Government to misuse it.

One of Voltaire's fictitious characters sought to discredit gold by producing handcuffs and other despised objects out of gold, in the hope that in doing so he could reduce the desire of the people to possess gold. Many more instances of similarly naïve attempts or suggestions could be quoted, but there are no instances in which the desired end was actually achieved. Gold remained a universally coveted metal throughout the ages, because through its possession its owners hoped to be safeguarded from losses through depreciation of currencies, through bank failures and through other contingencies. The desire to hoard gold tends to increase in many countries – even in advanced countries such as France – whenever threat of a war or a civil war or of a financial crisis creates a feeling of uncertainty. No amount of anti-gold propaganda can persuade the public that paper moneys or book entries are more dependable than solid gold. Even though the British people are not in a habit of hoarding gold, it is significant that the extent of the increase in the price of objects of gold since the war has been well in excess of the increase of its gold value and of its production costs. This fact speaks for itself.

Legislation between the wars and since the end of the last war was introduced in most countries to forbid or limit the export, import, sale, purchase and holding of gold coins or bars by private residents. All such legislation, like the precedents created by Lycurgus and John Law, was adopted, not because gold was unwanted or distrusted by the public but because it was wanted and trusted too much for the convenience of the authorities. In the absence of official discouragement facilities for hoarding would be used too extensively and would go a long way towards discrediting inconvertible currencies and paper credit.

There are admittedly some historical instances in which gold did go to a discount in relation to inconvertible currencies. During the First World War legislation was adopted in Sweden in February 1916 authorising the Riksbank to suspend its purchases of gold. As a result gold went to a discount against the Riksbank's notes. Commenting on this strange event, the leading Swedish economist Gustav Cassel observed in his post-war book *Money and Foreign Exchange After 1914*: 'For thousands of years gold has been the chief of all means of payment, and it was to be degraded and regarded as inferior to a purely paper currency.' The same situation had arisen in other neutral countries which, in an effort to mitigate the inflationary effect of their abnormally large balance of payments surpluses, sought to discourage the influx of gold. But soon after the end of the First World War, when Sweden and the other neutral countries ceased to suffer from an *embarras de richesse*, strong demand developed everywhere for the conversion of notes into gold, so that the Riksbank and the other monetary authorities concerned had to suspend the convertibility of their notes. The discount of gold gave way to a substantial premium.

The above long-forgotten isolated instances in the appreciation of paper money to above its gold parity – which I am giving herewith to the anti-gold school as a free gift – provides no valid arguments for a demonetisation of gold in the present situation. Sweden and other neutral countries had had huge export *surpluses*. On the other hand the United States felt

impelled on 15 August 1971 to suspend the limited convertibility
of the dollar into gold even for the benefit of official holders,
because of the gigantic balance of payments *deficit* and the
resulting accumulation of external short-term indebtedness
well in excess of her gold reserve. I am sure that, unlike the
Riksbank in 1916, the Federal Reserve authorities and the
United States Treasury would be still prepared to *buy* gold at
the old dollar parity of $35 per ounce, or at the new parity of
– notwithstanding their public assertions to the contrary – $38
per ounce, if anyone were foolish enough to sell any at that price,
and if they had a balance of payments surplus. But they are not
prepared to *sell* gold even at the increased official price, because
of their fears that the restoration of even a limited convertibility would deplete the gold reserve. The price of gold in the
free markets rose in fact well above $38, and its premium gives
some idea about the true extent of the dollar's discount against
gold. The official American contention that gold would gradually lose its monetary character and that 'paper gold' –
Special Drawing Rights issued by the International Monetary
Fund – is, or should be preferable to gold, does not carry much
conviction in the light of the existence of a premium on gold
in the free market.

Agitation in favour of de-monetising gold, and forecasts of
a decline of its value to that of scrap iron, are not a new phen-
omenon even in modern times. In the nineteenth century John
Ruskin argued furiously against gold. During the economic
depressions of the inter-war period Keynes and McKenna were
at the spearhead of the movement aiming at terminating the
monetary role of gold. They were opposed to the gold standard
on the ground that the discipline it had imposed on the economy
had prevented a credit expansion which would have reduced
unemployment. It was not discovered until the publication of
the Keynes papers in Vol. XIV of his collected works in 1971
that during the First World War both he, in his capacity of
economic advisor to the Treasury, and McKenna as Chancellor
of the Exchequer, were firmly convinced that unless the
pretence of Britain being still on the gold standard was upheld

her prestige and her financial power would decline to such extent as to make it impossible for her to continue fighting Germany. This was of course absurd, but it indicated the spirit of the times. Their change of attitude after the war was the result of inter-war depression calling for an expansionary monetary policy, the adoption of which was prevented by the need for credit restraint in order to maintain the gold standard on the basis of the 1914 parity of sterling. It is understandable that those two leading experts came to consider it imperative to range themselves against the gold standard in the then prevailing circumstances.

The argument that induced Keynes and McKenna to change their opinion and turn against the gold standard during the 'twenties certainly does not apply during the 'seventies. Ever since the outbreak of the Second World War – indeed from the beginning of rearmament shortly before the war – there has been an almost uninterrupted world-wide wage and price inflation. Had it not been for the relative stability of parities due to the operation of the Bretton Woods system this inflation would have proceeded at a much faster pace. It would proceed at a much faster pace if the remainders of the discipline imposed on the economy by the limited monetary role of gold under the realignment of parties on 18 December 1971, should come to be removed.

Even though today inflation is a much graver danger than deflation the majority of academic economists, which was strongly in favour of upholding or restoring the gold standard during the deflationary periods between the two wars, is now just as strongly in favour of abandoning it. The anti-gold movement has never been nearly as strong as it is at present. It is no longer confined to a few theoretical economists, to bankers anxious to expand credit, to businessmen wanting to borrow more, and to currency cranks. It is now supported by the Governments of the two Anglo-Saxon countries which had been the chief upholders of sound and conservative finance, and even by the West German Government which is in a strong enough financial position to uphold stable parities. While the British and American official attitude is an understandable symptom of the 'sour-grape complex' from which the two countries are suffering – they are against the gold standard simply because they both feel its maintenance is outside their reach – West Germany could afford to rely on gold at least to the same extent as France does. And yet while France is a firm upholder of the monetary role of gold West Germany has abandoned the monetary orthodoxy she had developed as a reaction to her disastrous experience in advanced inflation, and she is at the time of writing strongly in favour of floating exchanges. Among other important countries Canada, a big producer of gold, is against monetary stability based on gold. Switzerland is on the side of monetary conservatism, but surprisingly enough Holland's attitude has been distinctly less sound.

A high proportion of those wanting to de-monetise gold – possibly the majority – are prompted not so much by their desire to remove an obstacle to credit expansion for the sake of economic growth but by their desire to do away with the system of rigid exchange rates. This is the attitude of the German, Netherlands and Canadian Governments. In this respect, too, they enjoy the whole-hearted support of the majority of academic economists who would cheerfully sacrifice stability for the sake of accelerated growth – in the case of Germany mainly for the sake of avoiding exchange control.

There is no distinct line between the two anti-gold schools. Those who want to replace gold by book entries primarily aim at expansion but are also in favour of flexible exchanges because this would obviate the necessity of defending parities at the cost of sacrificing expansion. Those who advocate floating exchanges or some other form of flexibility do not overlook the increased possibility of expansion resulting from the adoption of the system of their choice.

Although the majority of bankers take the conservative line and are in favour of retaining monetary stability in terms of gold, a by no means insignificant minority has joined forces with other anti-gold campaigners. Consciously or subconsciously they may be influenced by their interests in achieving wider scope for speculation and for credit expansion. As for politicians, expanding currency without having to defend rigid support points makes it easier for them to bribe the electorate by making expansionary promises at the time of electioneering or when in opposition, and implementing some of their pledges when their side is in office. It suits their political interests to weaken the discipline imposed by the monetary role of gold on the economy and on public spending.

Having regard to the increased degree of growth-hysteria that has developed since the last war, it is no wonder that we encounter so much opposition to the maintenance of the monetary role of gold. While after the First World War, and even during the series of crises in the 'thirties, a return to the gold standard was considered to be the ultimate end, today very few people are thinking in such terms. Even most people who are in favour of the gold standard consider it sheer wishful thinking to expect their dreams to come true. Although President de Gaulle, inspired by M. Rueff, had advocated a return to the full gold standard, most others favouring gold would be content if the relatively limited monetary role fixed under the Bretton Woods system could be restored. Advocates of gold are on the defensive, while their opponents have taken very much the offensive.

It seems to be in accordance with the basic trend to adopt gradually less disciplined monetary and financial systems. This basic trend is not confined to the monetary sphere. In the sphere of public debt management too the same trend is noticeable. Until relatively recently it was the declared aim of Governments to repay the public debt, the increase of which through wars or other causes had been considered abnormal and temporary. Sinking funds had been set up to provide for the repayments which were also facilitated by conversion operations. Today nobody dreams any longer of repaying or even materially reducing the public debt. Indeed its gradual, and even not-so-gradual, increase has come to be taken for granted. Since the State is eternal it is considered natural for the State to borrow without any intent ever to repay the debt.

Likewise it has come to be considered a matter of course to favour a reduction of the discipline imposed on the monetary systems and on the national and international economy by the monetary role of gold. That role became curtailed long before the present concerted attack on gold. The next five chapters describe the stages of the decline of gold's role from full automatic gold standard to the Bretton Woods system.

CHAPTER FOUR

Departure from the Gold Standard

LONG before the monetary role of gold became the subject of concerted attacks by opponents of its monetary use, its predominant position in the international monetary system gradually declined. In fact, ever since 1914 the trend of its decline continued, even though it was interrupted from time to time by spells of short-lived revival.

Even before 1914 the number of countries which had been on the pure gold standard was very small. Britain, the United States and the Netherlands were certainly on the full gold standard, and so were indirectly a number of British and Dutch Colonies and Dominions. But the authorities of countries such as Germany or France did interfere on many occasions with the automatic working of the gold standard. When the Bank of France did not want to lose gold it availed itself to its right to pay out silver five franc coins instead of gold. When the Reichsbank wanted to attract gold it accepted delivery at its Hamburg branch, thereby greatly reducing the cost of shipment. No two countries interpreted the rules of the gold standard in exactly the same way. A number of countries maintained their exchanges within gold points with the aid of a variety of devices, without resorting to convertibility of their notes into gold for export, which was, after all, the basic principle on which the system was supposed to rest.

During the First World War the operation of the automatic gold standard came to an end even within the relatively limited sphere in which it had been functioning. Its end was not sudden. For some time after the outbreak of the war sterling and the dollar remained convertible, but, judging by the fact that the substantial premium on sterling over the dollar during the first five months of the war failed to attract large quantities of gold shipments to the Bank of England, the mechanism could not have operated freely. Later when sterling came to depreciate below its gold export point in relation to the dollar and to the currencies of several neutral countries it would have been obviously profitable to export gold. But while in theory the pound remained convertible in practice the Bank of England usually succeeded in 'dissuading' applicants from insisting on their legal rights, unless the withdrawal was for some approved purpose. Moreover, while there was no official ban on the export of gold for private purposes, shipping facilities came under Government control and they were not available for gold exports unless the shipments were for official or officially approved purposes.

Nevertheless, the fiction that sterling was still on the gold standard was firmly maintained. As we saw in Chapter 3 when the Government was pressed to abandon that futile fiction the Treasury was strongly opposed to such a step. In the United States, too, when she entered the war and the currencies of some neutral countries went to a premium against the dollar, the gold standard came to be suspended. On their part the neutral countries concerned suspended their respective versions of the gold standard by authorising their Central Banks to stop the purchases of gold.

After the end of the war the United States soon returned to gold, but other countries, former belligerents and former neutrals alike, took their time before they felt able to do so. Gradually during the 'twenties one country after another stabilised its currency in terms of gold – either at its pre-war parity or at a new parity – but it was a different form of gold standard. In Britain and in most other countries no coins were issued for domestic circulation, apart from other reasons because UK residents were not permitted to hold large amounts of gold. Although the Bank of England did pay out sovereigns for the purpose of exporting them, the monetary system that was in operation in Britain was not the full gold standard in the pre-war sense but what was called the 'gold bullion standard.' Bank of England notes were freely convertible for the purpose of arbitrage shipments, but these were increasingly in the form of bullion.

Other countries, too, departed to some degree from the pre-war rules of the orthodox gold standard. Gold legislation in most countries had some peculiarities – their detailed description by the League of Nations Finance Committee filled a fair-sized volume – and the application of the rules in practice differed from country to country. Nevertheless by and large there was a high degree of freedom for gold withdrawals and there were frequent gold movements between a large number of countries. There was a fair scope for banks and brokers engaged in gold arbitrage to resort to ingenious practices with the aid of which they could earn a profit on shipments as soon as the exchange rates touched their gold points.

But as far as Britain and most other countries were concerned the gold standard during its brief period of operation between the wars was not a pure automatic gold standard but more or less a managed gold standard. The way in which the gold standard is supposed to ensure the automatic adjustment of the balance of payments is through the effect of the influx or efflux of gold on the volume of credit in the country gaining or losing gold. As a result of this effect prices in the country with an export surplus tended to rise while prices in a country with an import surplus tended to fall, and this brought about a read-justment of the balance of payments. But during the inter-war period Britain and several other countries on a gold basis very often pursued policies aimed at preventing gold movements from producing their normal effect on the volume of credit. Unwanted gold movements were not actually prevented but their effect on the volume of credit was neutralised through mopping up unwanted liquid resources or supplementing deficient credit resources.

By such means the Bank of England prevented an aggra-vation of the depression that would have taken place if the outflow of gold had been allowed to produce its normal effect on the volume of bank credit. It sometimes also prevented an influx of gold from causing a credit expansion when it believed that the influx would be purely temporary and would be followed by an efflux, and especially when the influx was a purely artificial result of some ingenious device applied by the importer of gold. Thus when Mr McKenna, as chairman of the Midland Bank, sought to pursue his expansionary policy by importing gold on one occasion when it would not have been profitable to do so if he had allowed for the loss of interest on the transaction, the Bank of England simply neutralised the expansion of credit that would have normally occurred.

The gold standard became increasingly a managed system as and when co-operation between Central Banks became intensified. While there were occasional acts of co-operation also before 1914, in the late 'twenties some arrangements influencing gold movements came to be applied systematically. Thus a number of Central Banks got into the habit of keeping gold deposited with each other and whenever it suited their purpose such gold deposits were 'earmarked' against a credit in the currency of the country in which the gold was kept, or they were released when such credits were repaid. As a result it became possible to offset unwanted movements of exchange rates before they reached gold points.

This meant that the resulting changes in the gold reserves tended to affect the volume of credit in the two countries concerned before private arbitrage had a chance to carry out gold shipments. After the establishment of the Bank for International Settlements in 1930 this form of management of the gold standard became much more widespread and much more systematic. Central Banks participating in the BIS as its shareholders kept permanent gold deposits with it, and gold transactions between them assumed increasingly the form of transferring gold from one Central Bank's account with the BIS to another Central Bank's account with it. While some of the gold thus deposited was kept actually with the BIS in Basle, the greater part of it was kept with Central Banks in the principal financial centres where gold was considered to be the safest or was the most likely to be needed.

Such transfers of gold from one Central Bank to another through the intermediary of the BIS continued also after most countries suspended the gold standard in the 'thirties, so that there could be no more gold movements through private arbitrage. Had it not been for political developments culminating in the outbreak of the war in 1939 the functions of the BIS as the clearing house through which deficits and surpluses were settled through transfers of gold from one account to another would have become firmly established. As a result the operation of the gold standard would have assumed an artificial character, with international gold transfers carried out not when exchange rates reached their gold points but when it was considered necessary by the Central Banks concerned to increase or reduce their gold reserves.

Even such an artificial system would have been a form of gold standard, for it would have served the purpose of maintaining the external value of currencies stable in the vicinity of their gold parities by settling surpluses and deficiencies with the aid of gold transactions. But it would have been an artificial system. It would have constituted a major departure from the automatic gold standard in the sense in which it operated before 1914, and even from the gold bullion standard in the sense in which it operated for a short time during the late 'twenties and the early 'thirties.

Before this new system became firmly established it suffered a reverse as a result of the political tension between countries participating in it. The first event that came to interfere with the role of the BIS as a neutral and impartial clearing house was the surrender to the Reichsbank of the gold deposit owned by the Czechoslovak National Bank and kept partly in Basle and partly with the Bank of England in London. Even though later it became evident that the BIS had acted strictly in accordance with the legal position after consulting the Bank of France and the Bank of England, the controversy this incident aroused in 1938 came to inspire distrust in the BIS. The latter sought to prove its good faith after the outbreak of the war when it made a declaration of neutrality, giving an undertaking that it would abstain for the duration of the war from any transaction which would be to the advantage or disadvantage of any of the belligerent countries. In practice this meant that the gold deposits with the BIS became frozen for the duration.

As a result of this attitude the BIS proved itself qualified for resuming its role as the principal international clearing house for official gold transactions and for transactions between Central Banks in general. But largely owing to the repercussions of the Czech gold affair it was deemed expedient by the delegates who came to determine the post-war monetary system at Bretton Woods in 1944 to create an entirely new institution, the International Monetary Fund, to act as a clearing house between Central Banks. Instead of developing a managed gold standard a largely different monetary system was elaborated and was adopted after the war. It departed from the original gold standard even more than the managed inter-war gold standard, although it retained one of the basic characteristics of the gold standard – to maintain the exchange value of currencies within a narrow range around their gold parities.

Another device by which the monetary system came to depart from the pure gold standard was the adoption of the gold exchange standard in a number of countries. In a sense this was also a form of the managed gold standard. But owing to its importance we propose to deal with it in Chapter 6.

CHAPTER FIVE

End of Gold's Domestic Monetary Role

BEFORE 1914 the monetary role of gold was not confined to the international monetary sphere. It fulfilled an important role also in the domestic monetary sphere. In a number of countries the notes were freely convertible into gold coins and the latter constituted a high proportion of the monetary circulation. To a large degree confidence in notes was due to the fact that they were freely convertible for all holders into gold coins. Central Banks maintained substantial gold reserves not only in order to be able to meet international requirements but also in order to fulfil their statutory obligation to convert their notes into coins.

This phase in monetary history was a transitional phase between the period when coins constituted the sole circulating media and the more recent period when notes came to assume that role. In a number of countries notes were inconvertible, however, most of the time during the nineteenth century. The reasons why in spite of this such inconvertible notes were readily accepted for domestic purposes were threefold:

(1) It was widely if not generally hoped that sooner or later the notes would become convertible into gold coins or, as the case may be, into silver coins.

(2) It was generally assumed that notes accepted in settlement of claims could be used freely by their recipients in payment of their own liabilities.

(3) Notes were legal tender in their respective countries of issue, which meant that residents in those countries were under legal obligation to accept them in settlement of their claims.

In many countries the first of these three reasons had not rested on very solid foundations. Although the finances of the countries concerned improved from time to time sufficiently to enable their note issuing authorities to resume convertibility, sooner or later a war or some crisis, or just a deterioration of their finances, made it necessary to suspend convertibility and to reserve their gold holdings for meeting balance of payments deficits. Owing to such experience, the habit of hoarding coins became widespread, and in many countries coins commanded a premium over notes in domestic circulation. While in some instances, such as that of Britain during the Napoleonic Wars or in that of the United States during and immediately after the Civil War, it had been generally assumed that a return to convertibility was a mere question of time, this was not the case in the majority of instances.

The main reason why in spite of this notes were freely acceptable in domestic circulation unless and until inflation reached a very advanced stage was that the Government itself accepted them in payment of taxes and other dues, and that it made compulsory for private creditors or other claimants of payments to accept the notes in settlement of their claims. This fact gave rise to the so-called State theory of money, put forward by G. F. Knapp shortly before the First World War – that the acceptibility of money was based on the authority of the State. There is undoubtedly a great deal in his contention suggesting that inconvertible paper money is acceptable not because of convertibility prospects – which are at present exactly nil, at any rate for domestic holders – nor even because of the faith of recipients to be able to pass them on, but because they are lawful means of payment which must be accepted.

This assumption is well worth bearing in mind when considering the modern contention that just as inconvertible notes replaced in due course the gold coins in domestic circulation so SDRs may be expected to replace gold in international payments. It is true, increase of mutual confidence over the centuries may have had a great deal to do with the acceptability of inconvertible notes, apart altogether from the enforcement of their acceptability by legislation under which anyone refusing to accept a currency that is legal tender is subject to penalties. But it is fallacious to infer from this experience that further progress of mutual confidence must necessarily point towards the universal unrestricted acceptance of inconvertible international means of payment in international circulation. For the writ of Governments do not run beyond the borders of their respective countries. This means that there can be no such things as international legal tenders so long as countries retain their national sovereignties. While it is true that US dollar notes were widely accepted in Canada at their face value in stores or hotels so long as the disparity between them was fractional, Canadian dollar notes were not accepted at their face value in the United States nearly as freely. Most notes are not accepted in payment outside their respective countries of issue; they have to be exchanged at current exchange rates into local currencies. Likewise, it is a mistake to assume that the trend of evolution necessarily points towards the free unlimited acceptability of SDRs for the settlement of international liabilities even between Central Banks.

During the First World War the domestic role of gold came to be reduced in all belligerent countries and in most neutral countries. The issue of new coins to private holders of notes was confined to approved cases, and as a result of appeals to the patriotism of the people at war the greater part of privately held gold coins came to be surrendered to the Governments to assist them in their economic war effort. According to figures compiled by the League of Nations Finance Committee, the value of privately held gold coins surrendered to the authorities between 1913 and 1925 was $2,670 million. Even though several Governments resumed the issue of gold coins during the first half of the inter-war period, the crises and devaluations of the 'thirties resulted in a cessation of issuing coins and large amounts of gold found their way from private hoards into official reserves. The minting of sovereigns was resumed by the Royal Mint in the 'fifties, but solely for the purpose of exporting the much sought-after coins.

Under the system of the gold bullion standard Central Banks were nor required to convert their notes to resident holders. Nevertheless the fiction that their gold reserves served the purpose of covering the domestic currency and credit system and not merely of meeting balance of payments deficits was upheld. In most countries Central Banks were obliged by their statutes to maintain a certain percentage of their sight liabilities in the form of gold and/or foreign exchanges. This provision was based on the assumption that their reserves still played the part of note cover, even though the notes were no longer convertible for residents. In every country it was always assumed that all notes would never be presented for conversion at the same time, and Central Banks were therefore authorised to issue notes well in excess of their reserves. They had an authorised fiduciary issue as in Britain or they had a reserve ratio, a proportion expressed in percentage of the note issues and other slight liabilities. But even though part of the note issue was covered in theory by gold or by foreign exchange holdings was in practice not convertible for resident holders of notes, except for certain approved purposes.

Under the full gold standard gold coins circulated freely. Under the gold bullion standard they were available for export, but most gold purchases and sales by Central Banks assumed the form of gold bars. They were bought and sold by banks and by bullion brokers who were familiar with the specialised technique of these transactions. The costs would have been higher for those unfamiliar with the routine, so that long before it would have become profitable for them to operate professional operators restored the exchanges to within gold points as a result of their gold imports and exports. The stability of exchanges between countries on a gold bullion standard was not affected by the absence of gold coins in circulation or by the inconvertibility of the currencies for domestic purposes.

The inconvertibility of notes for domestic purposes became more evident and was made virtually permanent as a result of the difficult conditions created by the series of financial crises and the prolonged world-wide economic depression during the 'thirties. In 1931 and in subsequent years most countries which had been on the gold standard suspended the gold standard. And even after the *de facto* re-stabilisation of some currencies their currencies remained inconvertible. A large number of countries followed the German example and isolated the national monetary system from the international monetary system through introducing strict exchange control. These measures stressed further the essentially national character of the inconvertible notes. A similar system came to be adopted by other countries after the outbreak of the war when the surrender of privately held gold coins or bullion was made compulsory.

These measures virtually completed the demonetisation of gold for domestic purposes. Although under the post-war system the make-believe under which some Central Banks were holding gold reserves for serving as the basis of domestic currency and credit was resumed, it became quite obvious that the authorities restricted the role of gold or foreign exchange reserves to serving purely international requirements. This was made quite clear in the case of Britain, the country that originated the modern gold standard after the Napoleonic Wars. One of her first measures after the outbreak of the war in 1939 was the transfer of virtually the whole of the Bank of England's gold and foreign exchange reserve to the Exchange Equalisation Account. Even after the end of the war the Bank of England's own gold reserve remained purely nominal and the expanding volume of note issue and other short liabilities of the Bank was covered by frequent adjustments of the amount of the fiduciary issue.

In other countries, too, for all practical purposes the gold and foreign exchange reserves have ceased to be used or regarded as serving as covers for note issues and short-term liabilities. In most countries the security of these liabilities is ensured by the rule under which Central Banks' lendings must constitute well-secured self-liquidating short-term credits. As far as the domestic monetary system is concerned it is correct to state that gold has become demonetised for theoretical as well as practical purposes.

This change has come to be accepted as final and unalterable in most quarters. There are nevertheless still a few wishful thinkers who dream about the return to a system under which notes become once more convertible into gold coins. This school is particularly in evidence in the United States where there has been a persistent agitation by a small but vocal and not uninfluential minority in favour of the resumption of the issue of gold coins for domestic circulation. Indeed an attempt was made by a Senator when Congress was considering the legislation providing for the increase of the official price of gold $35 to $38, to introduce an amendment under which gold would be made available at its increased price for residents in the United States. Considering that the free market price of gold in London, Zurich and other markets was fluctuating at the time between $48 and $49, the adoption of the proposal would have meant that the entire gold reserve of the United States would have been withdrawn by private hoarders in a matter of weeks. Fortunately common sense prevailed and the amendment was rejected.

It is, or should be, quite obvious that the free world's existing monetary stocks of gold, amounting to some $40 billion, of which about a quarter is held by the United States, are far from sufficient even to cover international requirements. It would have been the height of irresponsibility to waste the American gold reserve for satisfying the selfish greed of would-be hoarders. The attitude of those who demanded a return to convertibility of the dollar for domestic holders may have been understandable when the American gold reserve was foolishly allowed to go down the drain for years in order to meet the insatiable demand of foreign hoarders and speculators who had been able to buy in the free market unlimited quantities of gold at the official American selling price of $35 plus minor expenses. The Central Banks' Gold Pool fully supplied the open markets, preventing the market price from rising above the official American price, and the United States had to provide 50 per cent of the gold required for that purpose. But this ill-advised practice was brought to an end in March 1968, so that spokesmen of would-be hoarders in the United States were no longer able to argue that non-residents were treated more favourably than American citizens resident in the United States.

The defeat of the foolish attempt to waste the American gold reserve for enabling domestic hoarders to satisfy their unwarranted demands for gold made it even more obvious that for domestic purposes gold ceased to play a monetary role. Quite evidently such monetary role as it was to play had to be confined to the international sphere. Even in this respect, the adoption of the gold exchange standard, of exchange control, and of the Bretton Woods system gradually reduced the international monetary role of gold.

CHAPTER SIX

The Gold Exchange Standard

WE saw in the last chapter that gold became virtually de-monetised as far as its former role in the domestic monetary sphere was concerned. But even its international monetary role was drastically reduced during the inter-war period largely as a result of the development and expansion of the gold exchange standard. Under that system the role that was formerly played by gold as a reserve and as a means of international payment is played partly or even wholly by holdings of foreign curren-cies convertible into gold or at any rate commanding a high degree of confidence abroad.

It is widely believed that the gold exchange standard originated at the Genoa Conference of 1922 which passed a resolution advocating the use of foreign exchange reserves by Central Banks to supplement their gold reserve. The object of this resolution was to reduce the monetary demand for gold, in view of the inadequacy of gold supplies available to meet that demand. The resolution came to be widely implemented during the 'twenties. It was embodied in the statutes and practices of a large number of Central Banks. It can therefore be claimed that the Genoa resolution has institutionalised the practice of using foreign exchange reserves to replace or rein-force gold reserves.

But the practice did exist long before the Genoa Conference. It developed and came to be widely employed during the nineteenth century. Indeed it is possible to find isolated instances for its use even in the eighteenth century. One of the first modern instances was provided by the terms of the Scandinavian Monetary Union of 1885, under which the

Central Banks of Sweden, Norway and Denmark kept balances with each other and granted credits to each other, thereby obviating the necessity of settling any surpluses or deficits on their trade with each other with the aid of gold transactions. Both Russia and Austria-Hungary maintained the stability of their exchanges not by means of official sales and purchases of gold but by means of official sales and purchases of foreign exchanges. To that end their Central Banks had to maintain foreign exchange reserves in addition to their gold reserves.

But even countries on the gold standard acquired the habit of maintaining foreign exchange reserves. Their holdings of foreign exchanges were in addition to their gold reserves which were always sufficiently large to conform to the statutory minimum requirements without having to reckon their foreign exchange holdings as part of these reserves. The main purpose of these reserves was usually to meet predictable official requirements such as the service of foreign debts, or to retain proceeds of foreign loans which were not required immediately. But in some instances Central Banks used their foreign exchange reserves to intervene in the foreign exchange market to prevent an unwanted depreciation of their currencies. In other instances they intervened to prevent an influx of gold because they wanted to avoid including in their gold reserves the proceeds of some temporary balance of payments surplus. Their object was to avoid an unwanted expansion of domestic credit which would have followed the increase of their published gold reserves.

Outstanding instances of the use of the gold exchange standard before the First World War included the use of sterling for international settlements by India since the end of the nineteenth century, and the use of US dollars by the Philippines after the United States gained control of that country. The international transactions of Japan and of the Argentine were based on sterling rather than on gold until the outbreak of the First World War.

Following on the Genoa Resolution the League of Nations Finance Committee ensured, when assisting various countries in their financial reconstruction, that the revised statutes of the Central Banks concerned should authorise the use of foreign currencies as parts of the official reserve. As already mentioned, the object of this policy was to prevent an excessive demand for the inadequate supply of gold.

After the stabilisation of the mark in 1924, the new statutes of the Reichsbank authorised the inclusion of foreign exchanges as part of the statutory reserve up to a maximum of 25 per cent. But as a result of the progress of Germany's reconstruction and of large-scale borrowing abroad the actual proportion of the Reichsbank's gold holding increased to well above the statutory proportion. From time to time the Reichsbank's actual holdings of foreign exchanges increased considerably, largely as a result of influx of foreign long-term or short-term funds, but most of these holdings were in addition to the statutory requirements.

Repatriation of national capital that had taken flight abroad was largely responsible for the increase of foreign exchange reserves of the *Banca d'Italia* and the *Banque de France* during the second half of the 'twenties. These movements were temporarily reinforced by speculative inflows of foreign capital. The size of the French foreign exchange holdings became particularly large after the *de facto* stabilisation of the franc in 1926. The Bank of France was anxious to convert these balances into gold and did convert a substantial part of them, but it was persuaded to retain part of its sterling and dollar holdings in order to avoid the effects of a reduction of the gold reserves of Britain and the United States. After the suspension of the gold standard in Britain the *Banque de France* converted most of its holdings, cutting its substantial losses in the process.

Any Central Bank which intervened in the foreign exchange market, or which adopted the practice of supplying import requirements and taking over proceeds of exports, had to hold foreign exchanges, if only temporarily. Most of them kept these foreign exchanges in addition to their statutory reserves as in the pre-1914 days, while others included them in their statutory reserves. The influx of foreign exchanges increased the volume of credit in the surplus countries and it also increased the international grand total of credits unless the receiving Central Banks converted the exchanges into gold, thereby preventing a duplication of credit.

The increase in the volume of credits was more substantial if the foreign exchange holdings formed part of the Central Banks' statutory reserve against which it was entitled to issue notes or expand credit to a total several times the amount of the exchange reserve. This was why the operation of the gold exchange standard was criticised, especially by French experts, as being a source of international inflation. If a Central Bank held in its statutory reserves currencies convertible into gold, the gold held by the country whose currency it held served as a basis for credit expansion in two countries. According to M. Rueff, the most persistent opponent of the gold exchange standard since the late 'twenties, the extensive application of that system had been largely responsible for the international credit inflation that caused overlending abroad and culminated in the Wall Street boom and the subsequent slump of 1929, followed by the crises of the 'thirties. But considering that this credit expansion had failed to prevent the world-wide deflation of the late 'twenties this interpretation of the origin of the crises is open to doubt.

The conversion of French foreign exchange reserves and the reduction or elimination of other official foreign exchange reserves as a result of the distrust caused by the depreciation of sterling in 1931 and of the dollar in 1933 produced a setback in the trend towards the increased use of the gold exchange standard. The setback was, however, temporary. The establishment of the Sterling Area resulted in an increased use of sterling as official foreign exchange reserves by countries of the Outer Sterling Area. Since sterling was no longer convertible into gold this system could not strictly be called gold exchange standard, but it was sterling exchange standard. Throughout the 'thirties increasing intervention by monetary authorities in the foreign exchange market resulted in the accumulation and maintenance of large foreign exchange reserves consisting mostly of inconvertible currencies, because the currencies that were still on a gold basis, such as the French franc, were not trusted sufficiently to be acquired and held as reserve currencies.

During the Second World War most currencies came under strict exchange control and the foreign exchange requirements of Britain were met through the realisation of foreign investments and through Lend-Lease. All foreign exchange transactions in Britain and in most other countries had to go through the hands of the authorities, a state of affairs which was already in operation in Germany and in other countries long before the war. The effect of exchange control, and of the resulting bilateralism culminating in exchange clearing is discussed in Chapter 8 which shows that a perpetuation of that system would have virtually ended the monetary role played by gold. But one of the main objects of the Bretton Woods Agreement was to remove any such artificial interference with free international trade and finance and to replace it by the dollar standard which became one of the forms of the gold exchange standard after the war.

Under the Bretton Woods system the dollar shared with gold the role of international currency, and the drawing rights arranged by the IMF for its member countries provided another international means of payment. At the same time sterling recovered much of its pre-war role of reserve currency and international means of payment. Although it was not convertible into gold and even its convertibility into other currencies was subject to limitations, countries of the Sterling Area and many other countries used sterling to a large extent as a reserve currency. During the 'fifties when sterling was blocked even for non-resident holders but was transferable between such holders, transferable sterling became one of the principal international currencies and was widely kept as a reserve currency not only by private firms but also by official holders, because it was widely acceptable for international payments in spite of being a restricted currency.

After the liberation of sterling for international purposes it continued to play the part of gold substitute in international trade and payments. This in spite of the frequently recurrent sterling scares. It was not until after its devaluation in 1967 that its international role declined sharply. Even then, thanks to the Basle Agreement providing dollar guarantees to official Sterling Area holders, it retained its role as a reserve currency to a reduced but not inconsiderable extent. Following on the improvement of Britain's balance of payments in 1970–71 London came to attract once more an increasing amount of non-resident holdings of sterling, well in excess of the amounts guaranteed under the Basle arrangement.

As in the 'twenties so in the 'sixties France embarked on a crusade against the gold exchange standard. This crusade, directed mainly against the United States, will be described in greater detail in Chapter 13. Having converted into gold most of her own dollar holdings, France endeavoured to persuade other countries to act likewise, denouncing the gold exchange standard as the root of most of the evils. Her spokesmen, General de Gaule, M. Rueff and M. Debré, missed few opportunities to stress the need for returning to the pure gold standard. And since it was obvious that the amount of monetary gold available was not nearly sufficient to abandon the use of the dollar and sterling as reserve currencies, the French spokesmen advocated a drastic devaluation of the dollar and of other currencies, so as to increase the book value of gold reserves sufficiently to do away with the necessity of using the dollar and sterling reserve to supplement gold reserve. As this policy was inspired by de Gaule's anti-Anglo-Saxon attitude rather than by economic considerations, it seems that the right measure was advocated for the wrong reason.

CHAPTER SEVEN

The 'Gold Insolvency Standard'

WE saw in earlier chapters that the monetary role of gold came to be reduced before the Second World War by the cessation of its convertibility for domestic purposes and also for international purposes, and by the adoption of the gold exchange standard. This chapter deals with the reduction of gold's monetary role since 1914 by the adoption of various methods of exchange-controls. It was done in both World Wars, especially in the Second World War, but it had been widely assumed that the measures adopted under the prevailing abnormal conditions had been supposed to be temporary and the ultimate end would be a return to freedom of international trade and payments.

In a large number of countries exchange control was adopted or maintained, however, in time of peace, both during the inter-war period and after the Second World War. Foremost among the countries which resorted to exchange and trade restrictions in the 'thirties was Germany, even before the advent of the Nazi regime. This was deemed necessary after the sudden withdrawals of foreign credits following on the failure of the Austrian Creditanstalt in 1931. Germany did not possess the gold and foreign exchange resources to repay the maturing credits and the withdrawal of foreign funds would have resulted in a sharp depreciation of the Reichsmark in the absence of adequate official support. Since the memories of the depreciation of the mark in the early 'twenties were still fresh in the minds of the German people and its leaders, the defence of the currency with the aid of tight exchange controls was considered a smaller evil. Accordingly, the gold standard was suspended in the summer of 1931 and external payments were blocked.

The prolonged crisis induced a number of countries, especially in Central and South-Eastern Europe and in Latin America, to follow Germany's example, though the nature and extent of the exchange control they had applied differed from country to country. Residents in the countries concerned were prevented from transferring funds abroad without obtaining license from the authorities. Foreign creditors and holders of assets were also prevented from calling their claims – hence the Standstill Agreement with the Germans and other debtors – or from withdrawing the proceeds of their assets. In a number of countries they were able to sell their various types of blocked currencies at a more or less substantial discount in markets created for that purpose. This system came to be known as 'multiple currency practices.' Even the proceeds of current exports to the countries concerned were blocked. Since these measures enabled those countries to maintain the artificial stability of their currencies in relation to gold by simply defaulting on their external liabilities Sir Henry Strakosch aptly named the system they adopted the 'gold insolvency standard.'

In the course of the 'thirties the exchange restrictions and trade controls came to be tightened as a result of experience in closing loopholes. Most of the countries that applied that system had more or less exhausted their gold and foreign exchange reserves, so that they would have been unable in any case to maintain the gold standard or the gold exchange standard. Since in prevailing circumstances they were unable to borrow abroad they had to confine the value of their imports to the proceeds of their current exports. The adoption of this system by a number of countries had reduced international gold requirements.

It is always tempting to try to make virtue of necessity and there emerged a school of thought which sought to provide theoretical foundations to the application of exchange control. Forestalling advocates of floating exchanges in the 'sixties and 'seventies, this school of thought professed to prefer exchange controls to free foreign exchange markets under the gold standard, on the ground that controls insulated their countries from the disturbing influence of trends in the world economy. They enabled the Governments to pursue policies that suited national requirements without being forced by an adverse balance of payments to abandon those policies. Thus Germany was enabled by the application of tight exchange controls in the 'thirties to pursue an expansionary economic policy that reduced unemployment. Later under the Nazi regime she was also enabled by it to finance her rearmament which under free exchanges would have been prevented by the adverse change in her balance of payments and the resulting depreciation of the Reichsmark. As a result of this experience the view came to be adopted in a number of countries that the gold standard should be abandoned for good, for the sake of retaining the independence of their insulated national economies from disturbing international trends.

It goes without saying that this attitude was confined to financially weak countries which did not possess the necessary reserves or borrowing capacity or current surpluses to be able to afford to maintain free foreign exchange markets under the gold standard or under the gold exchange standard. Freedom of trade and exchanges is evidently a privilege which only financially strong countries can afford amidst disturbed conditions. While during the nineteenth century and until 1914 countries which could not afford to maintain the gold standard allowed their exchanges to depreciate and fluctuate, in the inter-war period and more recently many weak countries preferred to try to uphold stability with the aid of controls.

Another manifestation of weakness during the 'thirties was the development of a trend towards bilateralism in foreign trade and payments in the place of multilateral trade and payments under the gold standard. So long as countries possessed reasonably adequate gold and foreign exchange reserves or were in a position to supplement their resources by commercial or financial credits or loans abroad it mattered little whether imports and exports between two trading countries balanced. The deficit on the trade between country A and country B was offset by the surplus of the deficit country on its trade with country C. But in the 'thirties the reserves of many countries declined to danger level and credits or loans were not obtainable. Country A had to ensure therefore that its trade was balanced in relation to country B, just in case it could not earn a surplus on its trade with country C.

This aim was sought to be attained either by bilateral trade agreements or by exchange clearing agreements under which imports were paid out of the proceeds of exports to the same country. If a country was unable or unwilling to import from the country in relation to which it had an export surplus its export surplus simply remained unpaid. Quite a network of exchange clearing agreements were concluded during the 'thirties and a by no means insignificant proportion of international trade came to be financed through this system. In the course of time a variety of refinements were developed by the contracting parties, such as triangular or multilateral clearing arrangements with the participation of more than two countries, or the extension of the arrangements to cover debt payments.

The popularisation and perpetuation of this system would have contributed towards the reduction of monetary requirements of gold. Amidst the conditions prevailing in the 'thirties the alternative to exchange clearing was in many instances a further contraction in the volume of foreign trade, since many Governments felt they could not afford to risk admitting imports unless they ensured that payment would only be made out of the proceeds of the exports of their countries.

It was tempting to regard the new system as an acceptable alternative to free trading under the gold standard, all the more as it tended to discourage the 'beggar-my-neighbour' policies which became very popular in the 'thirties. It was useless to force exports on other countries by exchange dumping and other means if those exports remained unpaid until the importing country in turn is enabled to increase its exports to the country with the export surplus. Quite candidly I felt strongly tempted to regard exchange clearing as a permanent acceptable system and not merely an emergency palliative, and I only became disillusioned when I came to realise how easy it was to misuse it in the way Nazi Germany had misused it in its trade relations with smaller countries of Central and South-Eastern Europe.

As the Bretton Woods system was based on the fundamental principle of free trade and exchanges, participants in the IMF had to undertake to remove their exchange controls. In the course of time most of the pre-war arrangements of controls, bilateral trading and exchange clearing disappeared during the post-war period, at any rate as far as nonresident accounts were concerned. Some of the economically stronger countries came to feel that they were able to afford to relax and even remove exchange controls also in respect of their residents. These countries included the United States, West Germany, Switzerland, etc. On the other hand, several economically strong countries, such as France and Japan, felt impelled to retain or restore a high degree of exchange control even after the improvement of their positions.

During the late 'sixties when sterling and even the dollar came under attack, Britain and the United States reintroduced some measures of exchange controls as an alternative to resorting to unpopular deflationary measures for the sake of improving their balance of payments. Under the shelter of exchange controls it was possible to delay these measures to some extent, and to defend stability with the aid of inadequate reserves. In that sense exchange control reduced gold requirements, though it would be more correct to say that it deferred the adjustment of parities or the adoption of 'tough' measures for defending them. Nevertheless, although it enabled countries to retain gold's role as a standard of value, in a sense exchange control may be regarded as an alternative to the gold standard. Its extensive application reduced gold requirements, not only because it obviated the necessity to pay out gold automatically but also because it reduced or eliminated imbalances of trade which would have developed under free trading and which would have increased the requirements of liquid reserves.

So long as the world's monetary gold supply remains in-adequate to meet expanded and expanding requirements it is arguable that exchange controls are a necessary evil in that they obviate the necessity of excessive adjustments of parities, at any rate for a while. In the long run their operation, by deferring necessary measures to restore equilibrium, tends to aggravate disequilibrium, so that sooner or later more drastic measures would have to be resorted to in order to restore equilibrium. But if a disequilibrium is obviously temporary and there are not sufficient reserves to fill the temporary gaps there is much to be said for adopting restrictions in preference to unsettling the national and international economy by resorting to parity adjustments.

CHAPTER EIGHT

The Bretton Woods System

FROM 1942 onward Treasury experts of Britain and the United States were actively engaged in planning the post-war monetary system. Later representatives of other Allied Governments also joined in the discussions, but all along the principal participants were the United Kingdom and the United States, represented by delegations headed by Lord Keynes and Mr Harry Dexter White respectively. Since Britain and the other Allies were certain to depend extensively on American aid the American negotiators were in a very strong position. They themselves were not free agents, for even if they wanted to make extensive concessions they felt inhibited from doing so by the virtual certainty that Congress would not endorse an agreement that would go too far towards meeting the British point of view. For this reason the Keynes Plan with its essentially expansionary basic character, and with its formula enabling deficit countries to cover easily their deficits out of the resources of surplus countries – a plan which anticipated the device of Special Drawing Rights – was a non-starter in the 'forties.

There was little or no difference between the opinions held in London and Washington about the imperative need for doing away with exchange controls and restoring free markets in exchanges, though the American negotiators laid more stress on a relatively early restoration of freedom. Likewise, the American negotiators strongly favoured the adoption of a rigidly stable monetary system and their British antagonists had to fight for each concession in favour of a somewhat higher degree of flexibility.

The system that emerged at Bretton Woods in 1944 was not

as flexible as Britain would have liked it to be for the sake of being able to defend herself against imported deflation. It was sufficiently rigid to justify criticisms on the ground that it virtually amounted to a restoration of a form of gold standard, in the sense of ensuring stable gold parities. This interpretation was firmly rejected by Keynes in the course of the lively discussions that preceded and followed the conclusion and adoption of the Bretton Woods system. In the House of Lords debate on the legislation introduced at the end of 1945 to implement the American Loan agreement, Keynes made the following remark:

'Those who think that this plan means a return to the gold standard are unusually silly. I say unusually because one cannot expect too much in matters of currency.' This was a thrust directed at me – I was listening to his speech from the Press Gallery of the House of Lords – because I was practically alone in opposing the Bretton Woods Plan mainly on the ground that it would amount to returning to a particularly rigid form of gold standard. The name of gold standard implies a system under which gold is the standard of value and exchange rates are kept stable around their gold parities. I feared a repetition of inter-war history – credit restraint for the sake of defending untenable parities, and imported deflation because of our inability to defend ourselves against its import by downward adjustments of sterling, as we did between 1931 and 1939.

Experience of a quarter century of the Bretton Woods system confirmed my view that in substance it operated in the same way as the gold standard. Parities were rigid and had to be defended by credit squeezes, just like under the gold standard, even though there was no free convertibility into gold nor free gold movements to offset balance of payments surpluses and deficits automatically. But during the course of that quarter century I arrived at the conclusion that Keynes was right after all in yielding to American pressure in favour of the adoption of such a rigid system. Had it not been for Bretton Woods rigidity most Governments in this country and in other countries might have virtually abstained from defending their parities whenever their defence would have necessitated unpopular measures. As a result prices would have risen even more deeply than they had risen and the pound would be worth today a bare fraction of what it was worth in 1945.

We had been all wrong in expecting that the Second World War would be followed by a period of deflation similar to the period that followed the First World War. What made all the difference was the policy of full employment, the Welfare State and, above all, the change in the balance of power in favour of the trade unions. As a result of these changes, Britain's economy after 1945 had a strong inflationary bias, reinforced by the inflationary attitude of both principal political parties in Britain. To the extent to which the Bretton Woods system handicapped the progress of inflation it was a blessing in disguise. Whether I was justified in regarding its adoption as a return to the gold standard may be open to argument. But in retrospect I feel we are all indebted to Keynes for accepting in substance the American proposals with a few face-saving provisions added to it, instead of insisting on a return to the flexible system that had been in operation in the 'thirties. At that time flexibility was needed because the main menace was deflation. After the Second World War excessive flexibility would have been a disaster, because the main menace was inflation and it would have escalated greatly in the absence of resistance to devaluation.

Since the main characteristic of the Bretton Woods system was the maintenance of a reasonably high degree of stability its operation mitigated the rise in prices and the cost of living. Owing to the pressure of excessive wage demands no system could possibly have checked the rise altogether. It is true, under the Bretton Woods system the rise in prices was much steeper than it had been during corresponding periods of the operation of the real gold standard before 1914. Even so, in the principal advanced countries inflation did not exceed its creeping phase until 1970 when it became accelerated. The Bretton Woods system had contributed towards maintaining the purchasing power of national currencies relatively stable in terms of goods and services, in addition to maintaining their stability to a high degree in terms of gold.

It was not so much the actual rules of the Bretton Woods system as the Bretton Woods spirit that had prevented too frequent devaluations and runaway inflation. Under the letter of the rules of the IMF there could have been many more devaluations than there were in reality between 1946 and 1971. Apart from the possibility of taking advantage of the escape clauses in the Bretton Woods Plan, the IMF itself was not rigidly opposed to devaluations, and most Governments might have been able to overcome its opposition whenever they were very keen on devaluing. But since under the Bretton Woods system, as under the real gold standard, devaluation came to be regarded as an admission of defeat highly detrimental to the prestige of the devaluing Government and of the devaluing currency, most Governments made more efforts to avoid devaluations as far as possible than they would have made if the Bretton Woods system had not been adopted. For better or for worse – that is very much a matter of opinion – the Bretton Woods system acted as a stabilising influence.

It seems doubtful if during the last quarter of the nineteenth century when the gold standard was widely in operation it would have been possible to prevent a world-wide rise in prices comparable with the one experienced during the quarter century between 1946 and 1971 if the balance of power had been as much in favour of the trade unions as it was since the end of the Second World War. It is also very much open to doubt whether the world will ever approach the old-type gold standard to a higher degree than it approached it under the Bretton Woods system.

Until the late 'sixties the operation of the system made it possible for most advanced countries to eliminate or greatly reduce exchange controls, which itself made the system comparable with the gold standard. We saw in Chapter 8 that it is possible to maintain a high degree of stability of exchanges with the aid of exchange control, trade control and various bilateralist devices. The maintenance of a relative degree of stability without such controls and without direct interference with the operation of the economy in the form of physical controls justified a comparison of the Bretton Woods system with the gold standard.

Is it justified to regard the Bretton Woods system as a form of gold exchange standard? To a very large degree the stability of exchanges was maintained with the aid of purchases and sales of dollars. Until the middle of the 'sixties the dollar was convertible into gold, at any rate for official holders, so that in this sense it was a gold exchange. Thus any currency which was convertible into dollars was indirectly convertible into gold for official holders. Since, however, it was inconvertible for private holders, and became less and less convertible even for official holders after the middle of the 'sixties, there is room for objection to the application of the term 'gold exchange standard' when describing the Bretton Woods system even before it broke down.

It would be more correct to describe the system as the 'dollar exchange standard,' not only because currencies were convertible into dollars rather than into gold but also because the dollar assumed the role of the principal currency for international purposes. But the main reason why the dollar came to gain such prominence was the maintenance of its fixed parity in relation to gold at $35 m. per ounce. As and when the dollar became less and less easily convertible at that parity for official holders, as and when the market price of gold came to rise well above the official American price, it became increasingly difficult to uphold the fiction that the dollar represented a fixed quantity of gold. Hence the wave of distrust that developed against it.

Given the fact of the frequent dollar scares the system of the dollar exchange standard became increasingly removed from the gold standard and even from the gold exchange standard which was based on confidence in currencies serving as reserve currencies. Even so, it must be admitted that by and large the period of 1946–71 came much nearer to the gold standard than the periods of floating exchanges in the early years after the

First World War and again during the 'thirties, or the periods of exchange controls during the First World War and before and during the Second World War. As and when the controls were removed during the 'fifties the Bretton Woods system was approaching the gold standard. Had it not been for the waves of distrust that came to be caused by the recurrent sterling scares and dollar scares, the Bretton Woods system might have become sufficiently consolidated to bear comparison with the old gold standard, or at any rate with the gold exchange standard.

In any event, the Bretton Woods system was nearer to the gold standard than the alternative systems which might have arisen if it had not been adopted – the system of floating rates or the system of controlled exchanges. In theory it would have been possible to revert to the gold standard itself. This at any rate is the view of M. Rueff who succeeded in converting General de Gaulle and the official French opinion. There is a school of thought even in the United States which advocates a return to the full gold standard. This is sheer wishful thinking, having regard to the inadequacy of the volume of monetary gold available to meet the monetary requirements of gold, greatly increased both by higher prices and by larger volume of foreign trade and of international credit. The French supporters of a return to the gold standard are at any rate sufficiently practical to realise that it is conditioned on a major devaluation of the dollar and of all other principal currencies. Unless and until the world is ready for such major operation the dream of returning to the gold standard must remain a dream, and the nearest approach to it would be a return to a system that is largely similar to the Bretton Woods system. This would necessitate a return of a limited convertibility of the dollar into gold. Failing that, the stability of the dollar and of the other leading currencies would be maintained through their convertibility into SDRs, always provided that SDRs would be freely accepted by surplus countries in payment for their surpluses.

This system would be much further removed from the gold

standard than the Bretton Woods system. While the latter ensured a fairly large degree of balance of payments discipline the
system based on SDRs would mean a minimum degree of
balance of payments discipline. It would mean the application
of the all-too-fashionable permissiveness in the monetary and
economic sphere. This aspect of the subject is to be dealt with
in the next chapter.

CHAPTER NINE

Monetary Permissiveness

THE late 'sixties and early 'seventies have been characterised by an all-round deterioration of discipline in almost every sphere of human relations, by an all-round demoralisation. Authority is no longer respected in a great many families, at schools, in factories. Violent demonstrations have taken the place of rational argument. There are systematic attempts of intimidation of silent majorities by noisy minorities instead of acceptance of majority decisions. Morals have become lax, doping and other misuses of the human body and mind have become accepted practices. In outward appearance young men and women outbid each other in their effort to try to look as disreputable as possible, if only for the sake of expressing their contempt for traditional standards of behaviour. Discipline has become a dirty word.

It is no wonder that in such a society discipline should deteriorate also in the monetary sphere. The rules of the permissive society have come to be applied also in respect of currency. The virtues of stability and security, like those of self-control in every other sphere, are hopelessly out of fashion and are denounced by those eager to swim with the prevailing tide. Taking the line of least resistance, living for the pleasures of the moment without worrying about consequences in the long run or even in the short run, has become the prevailing practice.

Inflation, like the taking of drugs, has become the accepted way of life. Although some of the less irresponsible quarters do make distinction between moderate and advanced inflation – as they make distinction between addiction to 'soft' and 'hard' drugs – they refuse to admit that advanced inflation is almost certain to follow its initial stages. Since early phases of inflation, like early phases of doping, are in many ways enjoyable to the addicts, those enjoying it don't want to spoil the pleasure of the moment by listening to warnings about the effects during more advanced stages. To recognise and admit the danger involved might mean an effort to impose discipline on themselves, or to accept discipline to be imposed on them by others. This would be the last thing they would want.

Since the monetary use of gold imposes some degree of self-control it has become unpopular. One can have a better time if one is not handicapped by the need for defending exchanges in the vicinity of their gold parities, and if one need not worry about balance of payments deficits, however heavy they may be, or about reckless overspending by Governments or by individuals.

The abandonment of stable currencies which is widely advocated and is frequently applied in actual practice is simply the manifestation of the same spirit that manifests itself in promiscuity and doping and drinking bouts, only on an infinitely larger scale. It is ever so much more convenient to let exchanges take care of themselves, to allow prices to rise, to concede wage demands, however unreasonable they may be, to run up heavy debts, public and private, for the sake of satisfying our desires to grab all that can be made available to us by adopting this irresponsible attitude. In retrospect it may appear foolish to the present generation to have submitted to any sorts of discipline in the past. Life is much more enjoyable if all discipline is discarded. The maintenance of currency parities and their defence against selling pressures at the cost of sacrificing or deferring the satisfaction of some of our desires would be swimming against the prevailing tide. Those who are vaguely aware that in the long run the cost of permissiveness will be heavy, shrug off the unpleasant thought by reminding themselves that in the long run we are all dead.

Hence the eagerness with which many Governments have seized upon the idea that, since the monetary use of gold imposes on us unwanted and despised discipline, gold must be eliminated from the monetary system. It is bound to be a popular line to preach and to practice, just as it is popular to preach and practice free love or to reject the right of our parents or teachers to interfere with the pleasure of the younger generation in any way. Why prevent them from enjoying life by trying to uphold outdated ideas, for instance that, in order to obtain a degree, they must pass examinations? It is much more popular to suggest that everybody admitted to a university should be given a degree as a matter of routine after three years of doping, demonstrating and fornicating. This at any rate was implied by the suggestion made by a Socialist Minister of Education while holding his responsible office, proposing that examinations should be abolished.

In the same spirit, why deny ourselves anything for the sake of preventing our currency from depreciating? Let the exchange rates find their level, it is not for the authorities to try to keep them stable and to expect us to make sacrifices for the sake of being able to hold them stable. Let prices rise without trying to hold them down at the cost of depriving.

Two generations ago the monetary circulation consisted of coins or of notes convertible into coins. Banking was subject to strict discipline, credits had to be well secured and self-liquidating, and banks had to maintain a certain proportion of liquid reserves. Today there is a gigantic inverted pyramid of unsecured non-self-liquidating credits. Until comparatively recently depositors and creditors had the benefit of safeguards, and there was solid gold with intrinsic value at the base of the pyramid. The golden foundation of the credit structure still exists, even though it now represents a much smaller proportion of the huge volume of credits. But for the sake of removing a further obstacle to permissive behaviour that foundation is now sought to be removed.

Now that mankind has become much less creditworthy, having discarded discipline that had safeguarded its solvency, it is adopting a system which implies a much higher degree of confidence in its creditworthiness. To lay down rules, to insist on safeguards would handicap growth and that is not

permissible amidst the prevailing growth-hysteria. An emi-
nent Professor spoke recently in a tone of contempt tempered
by pity about those out-of-date 'anti-social' people who are
prepared to slow down the rate of growth just for the sake of
ensuring the solvency of countries and, within the countries, of
banks and their customers. All this 'safety first' is a matter of the
past. Collateral securities, reserve ratios, and all that, are not
needed in our brave new world.

It is not surprising that in such an atmosphere the monetary
use of gold is now considered superfluous. In any case, it
has become fashionable to argue that gold has no great intrinsic
value, that it owes most of its value to its monetary role and
that as soon as its monetary role is eliminated its value would
be bound to slump. This was precisely what was said about
silver when its de-monetisation was discussed. Admittedly, the
price of silver did decline as and when its monetary role
ceased in a large and increasing number of countries. But today
its price is higher than it was when it was one of the two
monetary metals. Opponents of the monetary role of gold
hasten to point out that this is simply because in the meantime
the industrial use of silver has increased very considerably. But
can they be certain that if, as a result of its de-monetisation, the
value of gold should decline, the same experience would not
repeat itself? After all, even as it is, industrial demand for gold
has increased very considerably. It roughly equals the whole
new gold output outside the Soviet Union. Any substantial fall in
its price would be purely temporary, for it would encourage research aiming at discovering additional industrial use for it, in
addition to the increase in demand for its ornamental use. Gold
is a very attractive metal and has some unique qualities, and
it would not be too difficult to make more non-monetary use
of it if it should no longer be required for monetary purposes.

We are justified, therefore, in assuming that gold has very
considerable potential non-monetary uses. Having regard to
this, it is an absurd view that it owes its high value almost
entirely to demand for monetary purposes. But even if we
accepted that view for the sake of argument, it would be well

worth our while to uphold the 'fiction' of its intrinsic value because it does inspire some confidence. The intrinsic value of paper money, of securities, of ledgers into which our credit balances are entered, is equal to the price paid by paper mills for high-quality paper sold them by the ton for re-pulping purposes. Compared with that, the intrinsic value of de-monetised gold would be very high indeed.

But even if it were sheer self-deception to accept gold at its full face value, it is the kind of self-deception which benefits mankind. It does inspire confidence. What is even more import-ant, in fact much more important, its limited supply does impose discipline on us. Of course we could submit to similar discipline in a planned economy, especially if it is applied in a system of dictatorship. If the national economy were managed with the aid of five-year plans enforced by a Police-State there would be no need for the discipline that the monetary use of gold imposes on us. Under democracy, however, we do need some institution which maintains stability and tends to keep down our total demand to the volume of available goods and services. It prevents undue credit expansion which is liable to lead to runaway inflation or to speculative boom followed by slump.

Even if the discipline imposed by gold on the monetary system and on the economy is too loose – as it may well have been under the gold exchange standard and under the Bretton Woods system – it is better than no discipline. It may not be sufficient to prevent the development of a permissive society, but the removal of its limited discipline would greatly aggra-vate the conditions created by permissiveness.

For a more detailed discussion of the conditions resulting from the removal of discipline imposed on the economy by the monetary use of gold which ensures international stability of currencies the reader is referred to my book *The Case against Floating Exchanges*. Even if the monetary use of gold were confined to serving as standard of value in terms of which the national currency is fixed the need for maintaining its exchange value at its gold parities mitigates the development of an uncontrolled permissive society. This is achieved even if the currency is inconvertible, and even in the absence of a fully effective gold exchange standard. Of course for anyone in favour of permissiveness this is an argument against the use of gold even in such a limited sense.

CHAPTER TEN

Growth-Hysteria and Environment

ONE of the reasons why so many people are in favour of eliminating the last remains of discipline imposed on the economy by the monetary use of gold is the increasing extent to which this generation is affected by growth-hysteria. Politicians seek to gain votes by promising accelerated growth. Trade unionists insist that the Government must step up growth, without being prepared to contribute anything whatsoever towards achieving the ambitious targets they advocate. Economists out-bid each other in advocating, or at any rate wishfully forecasting, higher rates of growth. And the general public is duly impressed by the winners of this competition–those who outbid their rivals or opponents in their pseudo-scholarly calculations of the rate at which economic growth could or should or would proceed.

Nothing is easier than to play the parlour game of thinking of a figure, to double it and to add another point to it when seeking to convince the credulous public that they and they alone hold the secret of raising the standard of living at a satisfactory rate. It is always amusing to behold statisticians, economists, politicians and the TUC engaged in heated controversy whether the rate of growth should be $3\frac{1}{2}$ per cent or 5 per cent. As if the volume of the output were determined by learned calculations of the attainable rate or by figures put forward for the purpose of political propaganda, or even by policies adopted to escalate growth, and not by the effort put into their work by those directly concerned in production. When the TUC expresses its dissatisfaction over the inadequacy of the Governments' target and demands that the growth rate should be higher it would not think of indicating any willingness of

the unions to urge their members to work harder and thereby
to contribute towards the advocated task of increasing the output. It is blissfully oblivious of the existence of a flagrant conflict
between its advocacy of higher rate of growth and the multitude
of strikes, overtime bans, go-slows and other methods of slowing
down the rate of growth in an effort to secure more unearned
and undeserved wage increases.

In the old days the Government was admittedly in a position
to influence the rate of growth by pursuing an inflationary or
deflationary policy according to whether it wanted to sacrifice
growth for the sake of stability or *vice versa*. In such a situation
the monetary role of gold may have handicapped the Government in stepping up the rate of growth at the cost of a depreciation of the exchange and of the resulting depletion of the
reserve. But in prevailing labour conditions the influence of
monetary policy on the rate of growth is highly problematic.
The change in the balance of power between employers and
employees has made all the difference. Inflationary policy
changes the balance of power even more in favour of the trade
unions and their bargaining position becomes even stronger. As
a result wage demands tend to become increasingly unaccept-
able and even more working days tend to be lost through
strikes. For many years the virtual certainty of being able to
get jobs tended to reduce further the willingness of a great
many employees to put in a honest day's work for their excessive pay. There tended to be even more absenteeism, the men
preferring leisure even to additional earnings.

Although full employment no longer exists, the bad habits
it generated while it did exist continue even amidst increased
unemployment. The 'English disease' continues amidst inflation
and deflation alike – and it is not confined to its country of
origin – and is very much in evidence when inflation and stag-
nation are running concurrently. It provides a characteristic
example of the extent to which the existing self-contradictory
conditions have played havoc with textbook-rules. The reduction of the growth rate in the United States coincided with a
period of reflation. Nor was it sheer coincidence.

It is therefore far from safe to take it for granted that a replacement of gold by SDRs as the main monetary reserve, and an unlimited issue of SDRs, would necessarily result in an increase in the rate of growth, even if it should remove one of the obstacles to accelerated growth. It might not even prevent a decline in the rate of growth. But in fairness it must be admitted that on the face of it it might be reasonable to suppose that the mitigation of the need for credit squeezes and other devices taken in defence of stability under the present system does provide an opportunity for the stepping up of growth.

Even admitting that the elimination of gold from the monetary system would assist growth there remains the question whether an increase in the rate of growth is necessarily a Good Thing. Growth-worshippers have no hesitation to answer this sacrilegeous question in an emphatic indignant affirmative. But doubts are beginning to be voiced from an increasing number of quarters, many of them influential. For the connection between increasing rate of economic growth and increasing pollution and other forms of environmental deterioration has come to be widely realised. It is impossible to open a newspaper nowadays without coming across perturbing instances of pollution or some other form of deterioration inflicted on the environment as the logical consequence of the higher standard of living brought about by growth. Utter irresponsibility of those directly or indirectly concerned with increasing the volume of production regardless of consequences has caused the pollution of rivers and seas; it has poisoned the vegetation, the soil and the atmosphere. It has disfigured the countryside, ruining a large and increasing number of beauty spots. It has made life in cities such as Tokyo increasingly intolerable.

History severely condemns the Industrial Revolution for having left behind a heritage of ugliness. And yet the damage caused by the greed of industrialists and by the short-sightedness of the Central and Local Governments who had failed to prevent the creation of slumps and of repulsive factory buildings is not irreparable. Slums can be cleared, and have actually been cleared to some extent. Hideous factories can be replaced, and are being replaced, by modern buildings. But future generations will be unable to replace the fishes, birds and other creatures of the animal world which are being rapidly exterminated by the pollution of water, vegetation, atmosphere and soil which is proceeding almost unhampered. This process of deterioration has been greatly facilitated by the reduction of the monetary role of gold which has enabled mankind to increase the rate of growth before it has come to realise that the cost of impatient growth in terms of irreparable damage to environment is liable to exceed in the long run the benefit derived from stepping up the rise of the standard of living.

It is conceivable that if the continued monetary use of gold had slowed down economic expansion since the end of the Second World War, mankind might have had time to give adequate consideration to the environmental problems created by growth and might have adopted the necessary preventive measures to safeguard the environment even at the cost of slower growth. But in the absence of gold discipline in the economy short-sighted greed has prevailed and continues to prevail. Should the monetary role of gold come to be terminated altogether the destructive process will gather momentum. Admittedly there is at long last some progress towards the realisation of what is at stake. But this progress is very slow. Those who are trying to make public opinion aware that the price paid for the rate at which their possessions of consumer durables increase is very heavy are denounced and are sought to be ridiculed by demagogic growth-worshippers. They are up against the short-sightedness of the public, due largely to the not altogether disinterested attitude of many of those who influence public opinion.

Unfortunately the task of those who favour accelerated growth regardless of its effect on the environment is made easier by some of their opponents. The cocksureness with which some 'prophets of doom' forecast the exact rate at which pollution will destroy the vital amenities of the globe, and the exact time it will take to exhaust essential material and to make the globe uninhabitable naturally tends to discredit their prophesies.

It helps advocates of irresponsible growth to make the public think that all the fuss is grossly exaggerated and is the work of a mere handful of freaks who need not be taken too seriously. Of course the public is only too willing to allow itself to be reassured, since it means that they need not feel guilty about their own contributions to the process of deterioration. It suits them to believe that basically all is for the best and stop worrying about the tomorrow.

Although exaggeration is sometimes necessary in order to draw attention to development which would otherwise escape attention, the case for safeguarding the environment even at the cost of slowing down the progress towards a higher standard of living is strong enough without having to overstate it. Even without any exaggeration it should be obvious that at the present rate of progress the globe might become a very unpleasant place to live in unless mankind learns to practice more self-restraint in the satisfaction of its expanding needs and of its craving for luxuries. The application of a goldless monetary system will make it possible to accelerate the destructive growth. When it is too late it might be realised that SDR really stands for Speedier Doom Results. Once the proposed SDR scheme is in full operation it will be even more difficult for Governments and Parliaments to resist pressure for even faster growth at the cost of even faster environmental deterioration.

Nature provides in many spheres checks and balances for the benefit of mankind in the long run. Very often we fail to realise that those inconvenient checks and balances are really for our protection. It is indeed difficult to make people believe that there is a case for deliberately slowing down the rate of growth for the sake of safeguarding ourselves against pollution and other inevitable disastrous consequences of unduly rapid unplanned growth. Everybody is in a tearing hurry to exploit to the utmost limit the technological progress achieved during the present generation, for the sake of the immediate benefit this brings to manufacturers and their employees, to buyers of the increased variety of goods, and to the Government that claims credit for having raised the standard of living. Under a monetary system based on SDRs the temptation and opportunity for increasing these benefits will be even greater than it has been during the last decade or two. Under the gold standard growth was restricted as a result of the discipline imposed on the economy by the monetary system. Owing to the reduction of the monetary role of gold under the Bretton Woods system this restrictive influence diminished. And once SDRs come to be adopted under the new formula put forward by Mr Barber it will diminish further, for it will be possible to increase the volume of liquid monetary resources with a stroke of the pen. There is every reason to fear that the further weakening of discipline resulting from its adoption will step up the progress of mankind towards its ruin.

Likewise, the operation of a more flexible system of parities or exchange rates resulting from the termination of the monetary role of gold will further facilitate the acceleration of growth. The balance of payments discipline will be weakened further. It might altogether cease to exist. This is precisely what growth-maniacs want. If accelerating inflation is detrimental to the stability of exchanges, so much the worse for the stability of exchanges. There will be no more built-in discipline to handicap accelerated growth merely for the sake of keeping the exchanges stable.

How many people realise the vital importance of reserving a high proportion of our material and financial resources for the reparation of the very grave damage that has already been caused by the suicidal rush of mankind into ruin through excessive economic growth? To invent various methods by which pollution could be avoided and irreplaceable materials could be safeguarded, would call for a great deal of costly research. The application of the necessary devices would have to divert much productive capacity from the satisfaction of current demand to the task of safeguarding the future existence of mankind. This would necessarily mean a slower rate of growth. Indeed perhaps it might even become advisable to call a halt to growth for a time and even to put up with some temporary decline in the current output for the sake of dealing first with environmental problems before being able to afford to resume growth. Few politicians and even fewer economists have the courage to advocate such an unpopular course. It is much more popular to advocate devices that could speed up growth and blissfully ignore the adverse consequences. Those who seek to draw attention to the overwhelming importance of environmental problems are naturally less popular than those who recommend methods of accelerating progress towards higher and higher standards of living, even though it also means acceleration of our rush to our doom.

The amount of capital required for halting and reversing the trend towards environmental deterioration and for repairing the damage already caused – in so far as they are still capable of being repaired – would call for immense financial resources. It is indeed arguable that the issue of SDRs is badly needed in order to meet that extra demand. On the provision that the international inflation to be created by the application of the Barber Plan would serve mainly if not exclusively that purpose the case for an early adoption and extensive application of that plan would indeed be unanswerable.

On the face of it this contention might appear to conflict with my strong opposition to inflation. But my opposition to inflation is not dogmatic. I realise that in given situations inflation is admissible because it is the smaller of alternative evils. Thus if half of a country should be destroyed by a nuclear war, and even in case of some less extreme catastrophy, there would be a very strong case in favour of inflating for the sake of repairing the damage. Unfortunately the damage caused and to be caused by irresponsible growth is not nearly so dramatic as the damage caused by war or earthquake, or flood disaster, so that the imperative need for its reconstruction regardless of costs in terms of accelerated inflation is not nearly so obvious. But it is just as real. It deserves top priority in the determination of policies and in the allocation of resources. Let us have more SDRs by all means, provided that they are used for saving the environment, not for destroying it.

But in all probability the SDRs to be allocated when the

Barber Plan comes to be implemented will be used for aggravating environmental deterioration instead of financing the cost of its repair. They will finance the escalation of economic growth. It might take many years before the public could be made sufficiently conscious of the full extent of the danger of pollution and environmental deterioration to make it politically possible for any Government to call a halt to growth and to strain its resources to the utmost for making good the damage already caused. During those years the environmental deterioration is bound to continue. And the device of SDRs will be used and abused for financing growth, regardless of the resulting environmental deterioration. By the time Governments and the public will become sufficiently environment-conscious to make it politically possible to call a halt to growth and to concentrate on repairing the damage it had caused SDRs will have become too discredited by their excessive issues to be available for financing the cost of repairs.

This will mean that by the time mankind will have come to its senses it will be short of financial resources needed for pursuing the sensible course. It is too much to expect that the Governments will be capable of a sufficient degree of self-restraint to moderate the misuse of SDRs for further inflationary growth, so that the financial resources they represent would remain in reserve for financing the cost of repairing the damage environment. The availability of that inflationary device when mankind is still much more growth-minded than environment-minded will greatly increase the extent of the damage to be repaired eventually for the sake of survival, and it will reduce the resources that will be available for repairing the damage.

It must be borne in mind that SDRs can only be used extensively in an atmosphere of mutual confidence. That mutual confidence will be destroyed by excessive use of SDRs for financing accelerated growth. It is a fatal mistake to imagine that the sky is the limit to the extent to which SDRs would be accepted by surplus countries from deficit countries in payment for their surpluses. This aspect of the problem was discussed in detail in my book *The Destiny of The Dollar*. Here let it be sufficient to utter a warning that, should SDRs come to be discredited it would take at least another generation before an adequate degree of mutual confidence could once more be achieved. Evidently, removal of the remains of gold discipline by leading to an excessive use of SDRs for financing growth is liable to destroy the chances of mankind for financing the costs of reversing the deterioration of the environment.

Sooner or later the monetary role of gold might be restored. But by that time environmental deterioration might have gone too far, so that even a return to monetary discipline would be unable to repair much of the damage.

CHAPTER ELEVEN

The Market Price of Gold

So long as the number of leading countries were on the gold standard the market price of gold was of relatively small importance. Admittedly in countries such as India where the hoarding habit was prevalent the market price was apt to rise well above the official price. But most of the newly produced gold found its way to the vaults of Central Banks or to the markets where its price could not deviate to any large extent from the official price. After the suspension of the gold standard in the 'thirties there was a great deal of private de-hoarding, but the privately held gold that found its way to the market was easily absorbed by Central Banks anxious to replace their foreign exchange reserves by gold. Even though it became more profitable to produce gold owing to its higher price, most gold-mining companies took advantage of the higher price for concentrating on the exploitation of their low-grade ore deposits the working of which became profitable, in order to keep the high-grade ore deposits in reserve and thereby to prolong the life of their goldfields. For this reason the output did not increase materially in spite of the stimulus of the higher gold price.

The maintenance of the official price of gold at an artificially low level after the Second World War in spite of the rise in prices and in the cost of production resulted in an increase of the hoarding demand and also of the industrial demand. Until 1968 it was the official policy of the United States and of several other countries to prevent a rise in the market price of gold above the official American price of $35. Accordingly, in 1961 a Central Banks' Gold Pool was formed, with the object of maintaining the market price of gold in the close vicinity of the official American price. The United States initiated the Gold Pool and participated in it to the extent of 50 per cent, while the other 50 per cent was divided up between the monetary authorities of Britain, France, Germany, Italy, Switzerland, the Netherlands and Belgium. The Bank of England was in charge of the operations.

For a long time the Gold Pool operated both ways. A large part of the newly mined gold from South Africa and other gold producing countries was bought by the Bank of England on account of the Pool. The substantial quantities of Soviet gold which were sold during the first half of the 'sixties also found their way to the London market and through it to the Gold Pool. For years the operation of the Gold Pool resulted in the addition of gold to the reserves of the participating Central Banks. The Bank of England's net purchases on behalf of the Gold Pool were divided up among the participating Central Banks in proportion of their quotas.

The situation underwent an abrupt change in 1965, as a result of France's attack on the dollar about which more will be said in Chapter 13. Not only did the bank of France convert most of its holdings of dollars into gold but official French spokesmen embarked on a persistent campaign to induce other Central Banks to follow the example. This gave rise to a wave of distrust in the dollar and there was a considerable increase in private demand for gold. Both in 1965 and in 1966 the Gold Pool operated with a deficit, its sales exceeding its purchases. The participating Central Banks had to contribute towards meeting the excess sales out of their reserves in proportion of their quotas. In addition, the Soviet Union ceased to sell gold, partly because it became possible for her to obtain credits that went a long way towards financing her import surplus, and partly because she came to expect an increase in the price of gold.

In 1967 the Bank of France withdrew from the Gold Pool, which meant that the remaining Central Banks had to increase their participations in its gold deficits. Notwithstanding this, they continued to co-operate with the United States in an effort to keep down the market price of gold in face of heavy private hoarding demand. The United States Government came to consider it a point of honour to maintain the market price in the vicinity of the official American price, regardless of the loss of gold involved. In numerous public pronouncements, official American spokesmen pledged their country to the prevention of a rise in the market price of gold and declared themselves ready to resist a rise 'to the last dollar' of their gold reserve. This in spite of the fact that French and other withdrawals and the deficit of the Gold Pool made heavy inroads in the American gold stock.

There can be little doubt that the 'gold rush' contributed to some extent to the sterling scare that developed in the autumn of 1967, even though the main cause was the resumption of wage increases in excess of productivity after the termination of the wage freeze and of the wage restraint that followed it. It became obvious that the Labour Government was no longer able or willing to keep down wage inflation, and that the resulting adverse balance of payments was bound to undermine the defences of sterling. It became more difficult for Britain to continue receiving financial support from abroad, especially as the French Government came to dissociate itself openly from the rescue operations. The United states had to bear the lion's share of the burden. Even though she could ill afford it, she could afford it even less to allow sterling to be devalued, because it required little prophetic foresight to predict that, once sterling's defences have crumbled the international speculative attack would be focused on the dollar.

Following on the devaluation of sterling in November 1967 this was indeed what did happen. The storm centre shifted from Britain to the United States. A high proportion of speculation against the dollar assumed the form of hoarding gold or purchasing it for forward delivery. Since those banks or bullion brokers who sold gold forward covered their positions by buying a corresponding amount for immediate delivery the result of both forms of operations was buying pressure in the gold market and the excess of demand over supply had to be covered out of the reserves of the Gold Pool.

To anyone with a modicum of common sense it was glaringly obvious that the Central Banks could not cover the deficiency indefinitely. Yet the United States authorities refused to heed advice to abandon the hopeless struggle. They came to consider it a matter of prestige to maintain not only the official American price of gold but also the market price. They were able to persuade their partners in the Gold Pool to continue to contribute their respective shares in the loss, but several Central Banks were becoming increasingly reluctant to pour more gold into the bottomless sink that swallowed it. They did not share Washington's firm conviction that if only they held out the money available for hoarding and speculation would become exhausted long before their gold supplies became exhausted.

Having to waste large amounts of gold to meet private hoarding and speculative demand, the American authorities became increasingly reluctant to convert official holdings of dollars. They did not want to suspend formally the convertibility of these officially held dollars but they used all their influence to dissuade applicants from insisting on their rights. In many quarters this attitude was considered both inconsistent and unfair. While the American authorities had evidently enough gold to meet demand by private hoarders and speculators all over the world they were unwilling to carry out the undertaking they gave to the IMF in 1946 to convert into gold official holdings of dollars. By the spring of 1968 it became obvious that this state of affairs could not continue, because several Central Banks were on the point of following the French example, which would have made the burden on the remaining members of the Gold Pool intolerable. Yet American official spokesmen, and even spokesmen of members of the Gold Pool in conference assembled at Basle in March 1968, reasserted their firm determination to continue the futile exercise.

Just a week after the last of these official pronouncements it was decided at a meeting held in Washington on 18 March 1968 to dissolve the Gold Pool and allow the market price to find its own level. At the same time they were at pains to convey the impression that gold was, after all, 'sour grapes.' While a few days earlier they were ready to defend the market price with the last drop of their blood now they wanted the world to believe that gold was of no importance and they had not the slightest desire to replenish their depleted gold reserves through purchases in the market. The new creed that gold had ceased to be important in the monetary system might have carried more conviction if in the same breath the Central Banks concerned had not threatened to blacklist every Central Bank which would sell gold in future in the free market. They declared their intention to abstain from selling gold to any Central Bank which would sell gold in the market. Using its still considerable influence with the IMF, the United States Government brought pressure to bear on all Governments and Central Banks to keep aloof from the free markets that developed in London and in Zurich.

The result of this change was the development of a 'two-tier market,' with two sets of prices. The official selling price of the Federal Reserve and of the few Central Banks which were willing to sell gold remained unchanged, but there was a totally independent market price which after an initial rise came to fluctuate freely and at times very irregularly.

The fears that Central Banks might be unable to resist the temptation to snatch a profit by selling their gold in the free market were without foundation. The two main producers, South Africa and the Soviet Union, decided to abstain from selling in the market, in the hope that the resulting rise in the price would force the hands of the United States and the dollar would be devalued. But contrary to widespread expectations the market price remained under $44 in 1968. In the following year the sharp rise in interest rates made it too costly to speculate on the rise in the American price of gold, and many hoarders and speculators closed their accounts. There was consequently a sharp fall in the market price, and it was accentuated by the decision of South Africa to resume her gold exports in order to meet her balance of payments deficit. She did not want to depress the market price by selling her gold there, so she offered it to the IMF at the official price under the rules of which institution she was entitled to buy from it foreign currencies against payment in gold. But under American pressure the IMF refused to carry out this obligation, putting forward some unconvincing excuse to wriggle out of its commitment.

By 1970 the market price was down to the official American selling price and declined even somewhat below it. It remained low for some time. But the dollar scares of 1970 and 1971 revived expectations of an early devaluation of the dollar and the market price of gold responded to speculative demand. The revaluation and upward floating of various strong currencies, both before and after the suspension of the convertibility of the dollar on 15 August 1971, mitigated the speculative expectations of a devaluation, on the assumption that these revaluations and appreciations would obviate the necessity for the dollar to be devalued or at any rate they would greatly mitigate the extent of its devaluation. Nevertheless, there remained a widespread feeling that the mini-devaluation of the dollar on 18 December 1971 was not the last word said on the subject and that a major devaluation was a mere question of time. Hence the substantial rise in the market price of gold.

When it was found that the realignment of currencies failed to improve the balance of payments of the United States to a sufficient extent, and that Mr Nixon was stepping up inflation to reduce unemployment, there was another dollar scare early in 1972 and the price of gold rose well above $50 in May. Although pessimism about the dollar's prospects continued to prevail, and the sharp fall in interest rates made it less costly to hoard gold or buy it for forward delivery, expectations of an early devaluation came to be abandoned. But the price of gold remained firm because of increased industrial demand.

A great many operators took it for granted that in the long run the price of gold was bound to rise much higher. The question is, will the rise in the market price force the hands of the United States Government to embark on a major devaluation? In itself it is unlikely to do so, but it was widely expected that combined with an inflationary rise in domestic prices and the resulting aggravation of the balance of payments position, it might make the American authorities and Congress realise that there is no other way out.

Towards the end of March 1972, inspired rumours found their way into circulation about the alleged intention of the United States Treasury to sell a substantial part of its gold stock in the market, partly to take advantage of the high price, partly to convince world opinion about the seriousness of its intention to demonetise gold, and above all in order to reduce the embarrassing premium of the market price over the official American price. Beyond doubt, the fact that there were many ready buyers of gold at more than $10 above the official American price indicated the degree of distrust in the dollar at its devalued level, and it was reasonable to assume that the elimination or substantial reduction of the premium would make it easier to maintain the dollar at $38.

But the view was widely held that the dissemination of these rumours was sheer bluff. For one thing it was an open secret that the Pentagon was strongly opposed to a further substantial reduction of the gold stock, whether it was sold at $35, or at $38, or at a higher price. Besides, the sale of the American gold reserve in the market would cause very considerable resentment among Central Banks holding dollars, having regard to the fact that the United States Treasury unilaterally suspended the conversion of these dollars at the official price. The United States was no longer in a strong enough position to be able to afford to ignore the opinion of leading Central Banks, apart from other reasons because they had the power to veto the adoption of the Barber Plan on which the restoration of the strength of the dollar largely depended. Indeed it was widely suspected that the United States Treasury was spreading the rumour of its intention to sell gold in the market in order to bring pressure to bear on the Western European Governments and on the Japanese Government to induce them to proceed more speedily with the consideration of the SDR scheme.

There could be little doubt that even a comparatively moderate official American selling of gold would cause a sharp relapse in the market price. But such a decline would stimulate hoarding demand and it might induce a number of Central Banks to unload their inconvertible dollars in exchange for gold. So far from contributing towards the demonetisation of gold, the exercise would go some way towards assisting in the maintenance of its monetary role by correcting the existing maldistribution.

A unilateral abandonment by the United States of the rules agreed on 18 March 1968 and on 18 December 1971 would relieve all other participants in the agreements from observing the rules. Many Central Banks would undoubtedly arrive at the conclusion that the reduction of the market price of gold to, say, $40 through American sales would provide them with an opportunity for replenishing their reserves at a relatively favourable price. The psychological advantages that would be gained by the dollar would be purely temporary, as the market price of gold would rise once more as soon as the American gold reserve has become reduced to a level beyond which it is not expected to be reduced. For one thing, the prospects of the dollar would be viewed with pessimism because of the weakening of the American gold reserve and because it would be assumed that other Central Banks would no longer consider it their moral obligation to continue to bolster up the dollar.

CHAPTER TWELVE

The Purchasing Power of Gold

THE future prospects of gold depend not only on the extent of its monetary use and on its value in terms of current monetary units but also on the purchasing power of the current monetary unit in terms of goods and services. During various periods in the nineteenth century its qualification for serving as a monetary unit was contested on the ground that it was unstable in terms of goods and services. Each time after a major discovery of new gold deposits when the increase in the quantity of monetary gold was followed by a rise in prices, or when the demonetisation of silver caused scarcity of money and a fall in prices, the question was raised whether gold was adequate as a standard of value.

In a little-known work by W. Stanley Jevons called *A Serious Fall in the Value of Gold Ascertained*, published in 1863 soon after the gold discoveries in California produced their effect on the level of prices, rejected the contention that, owing to the inadequate stability of the value of gold it should be demonetised. 'The greatly multiplied mass of gold in use, the increased area of production, and the greater variety of nations which share in its production, will finally render it far more steady in value even than it has been.'

Of course in 1863 Jevons was thinking in terms of the automatic gold standard under which price levels adjusted themselves speedily and to a high degree to the changes in the gold output. In the meantime nature's influence on the determination of the price level through changes in the gold output was largely replaced by man-made rules in the form of the managed gold standard, gold exchange standard and the

Bretton Woods system, all of which reduced the influence of the gold output on its value in terms of goods and services. The changes in its value after the major discoveries of the past – or, for that matter, after the influx of gold from the New World during the sixteenth century or after the demonetisation of silver in the nineteenth century – were moderate compared with the change in its value since the 'thirties.

Although the increases in the gold output resulting from the exploitation of new gold deposits, and the movements of hoarding and de-hoarding constituted important factors determining the purchasing power of gold, monetary policy decisions are now incomparably more important.

The relationship between the general price level and the cost of production of gold is no matter of simple arithmetic, so that the rise in the price level without any corresponding rise in the monetary value of gold need not necessarily reduce the output as a result of the increase of the cost of production. For one thing, the cost of production of gold need not keep pace with the general rise in prices. Technical inventions and their increasing application are apt to affect the cost of production independently of the effect of the trend in the price level on wages. Another important factor is the policy pursued by gold producers. As we already pointed out, in the thirties the increase in the price of gold in terms of dollars and other currencies did not result in an immediate corresponding increase in the output, because many gold mining companies took advantage of the higher prices for switching their productive efforts on low-grade ore deposits the exploitation of which was not profitable prior to the rise in the price of gold.

Nature always plays a part not only in determining the output but also in determining the cost of gold production. The discovery of new goldfields where gold is more easily accessible and can therefore be produced at a lower cost is liable to be an important factor. Last but by no means least, Governments have a great influence on the quantity and cost of gold production, through the application and modification of taxation affecting gold mining and through their attitude towards the sale of gold in unofficial markets where their price is higher.

As far as gold production in the Soviet Union is concerned, the cost is irrelevant. We shall see in Chapter 14 that if the Soviet Government wants to increase the output in order to export more for the sake of meeting a balance of payments deficit, or in order to accumulate a large gold reserve, commercial considerations which influence privately-owned goldfields are ignored.

American resistance to adapting the price of gold to the rise in the price level was largely responsible for the decline of its purchasing power in terms of goods and services since 1934. If the United States Government should succeed in resisting a major devaluation of the dollar and in inducing other Governments to revalue their currencies this policy would lead to a further decline in the purchasing power of gold, since it is safe to assume that prices of goods and services will continue to rise possibly at a more moderate pace, in spite of the revaluation of some currencies even though the price of gold in revalued currencies is reduced.

In considering the destiny of gold it is necessary to envisage the possibility of a very considerable decline of its purchasing power as a result of the rise in the price level unaccompanied by corresponding adjustments of the price of gold in terms of monetary units. It is conceivable that gold might follow the fate of silver during the prolonged period when the output increased while its monetary use declined It is by no means outside the realm of possibility that gold might lose much of its scarcity value just as silver did in the late nineteenth century and the early twentieth century. There is no means of knowing whether additional rich and easily accessible deposits will not be discovered. Even though the possibility of inventing the production of synthetic gold may safely be dismissed, the possibility of a very considerable increase in its natural output should not be ignored. Should the annual output come to represent a high proportion of the existing monetary stock of gold it would justify resistance to the increase of its price in terms of dollars or other leading monetary units.

But it is conceivable that the increase in the price of gold will continue to be resisted even in the absence of an escalated increase in its output. To the extent to which the cost of production of gold follows the rise in price level this might tend naturally to keep down the output – except possibly in Communist countries.

But, as we pointed out earlier, it is safe to expect that in such situations the relative cheapness of gold compared with other commodities would greatly increase its non-monetary use. Owing to its beauty and its attraction for many people its ornamental use would increase considerably, and so would gold hoarding. Research institutions and departments would invent additional industrial use for it. As already pointed out, it is even conceivable that gently increased industrial demand and hoarding demand resulting from additional non-monetary use that would follow a decline in the value of gold would produce a similar effect as the decline in the value of silver did. The resulting non-monetary demand might raise its value above the level where it stood before its demonetisation.

In any case it is probable that continued resistance to the increase in the monetary price of gold might lead to the increase of its non-monetary use, leading to an increase in its intrinsic value. This again might make it more attractive for monetary use, since the world would realise that the value of gold does not depend, after all, entirely on its monetary use.

It is also conceivable that continued maintenance of an artificially low official price of gold, a price which is entirely out of touch with the rise in the level of prices, will lead to a widening of the discrepancy between the official and unofficial prices of gold. There has been a wide discrepancy most of the time since the establishment of the two-tier system in March 1968. Long before that there was a much higher black-market price in India and in other countries where gold is extensively used for hoarding and for ornamental purposes. In countries where gold hoarding is effectively prevented the price of gold objects rises well above the metallic value of their gold contents plus the cost of the workmanship and its artistic value. The more artificially low the official price is the more the unofficial price will tend to adapt itself to the rise in the general price level, through a widening discrepancy between official and unofficial gold prices.

This trend is liable to become much more obvious if a two-tier foreign exchange market should develop in dollars. There is already such a market in France owing to the differentiation between the 'commercial franc' which is subject to intervention by the Bank of France, and the 'financial franc' which is left to its own devices. If a world-wide two-tier market should develop in 'commercial' dollars originating from genuine commercial transactions and 'financial' dollars originating from speculation, flight of capital, arbitrage, export of capital etc., there might be some connection between the rate of the financial dollar and the market price of gold. In such a situation it is conceivable that a considerable depreciation of the financial dollar in the absence of its support by the Central Banks might entail a corresponding rise in the market price of gold.

Any effort to keep the price of gold at an artificially low official level is not likely to affect the ultimate destiny of the gold, which points towards a rise of its value to at least the same extent as the rise in the price level. Should attempts be made to reduce its price by unloading official reserves in the unofficial markets – which would have to be a very gradual process if official holders want to keep the resulting losses on their gold stocks down to a minimum – unofficial demand would gradually absorb the supply, so that any fall in the price would be temporary. Over a period of time hoarding and industrial demand would be capable of absorbing the monetary gold stock, even if the whole of it, totalling some $40 billion were to be unloaded in addition to absorbing the current output. But in any case a large number of countries would not demonetise their gold reserves, so that the supply to be absorbed would be much smaller. And several Governments would actually take advantage of the demonetisation of gold by other Governments for replenishing their gold reserves at a lower cost while the going is good. They would be safe to assume that the first major political or financial crisis would reverse the trend of the price of gold. Wholesale hoarding would then cause a sharp rise, especially if some leading currencies should come under a cloud and no other currencies would be trusted sufficiently to attract flight money.

In any case an increasing number of Governments have adopted or will adopt measures to discourage an influx of unwanted foreign funds. These would then seek refuge in gold, and the resulting urgent demand might cause a spectacular rise in the market price. This might induce many Governments to change their attitude and to revert to gold. It is reasonably safe to assume that the first major panic would create a situation which would utterly discredit the anti-gold school. Those Governments and Central Banks which had unloaded their gold reserves at a loss would then feel utterly foolish and would have every reason to regret having allowed themselves to be misled by doctrinaire opponents of the monetary use of gold.

CHAPTER THIRTEEN

The Franco-American 'Cold War'

REPEATED reference was made in earlier chapters to the French attitude towards the monetary role of gold during the inter-war period and again in the 'sixties. There is certainly a high degree of consistency in French gold policy. On repeated occasions France became the supreme defender of the monetary role of gold. While during a great part of the inter-war and post-war period her own domestic financial troubles prevented her from wielding much influence in the shaping of the international financial system, whenever she staged a recovery she threw herself wholeheartedly into the crusade for maintaining and increasing the importance of gold in the monetary system.

This consistency of the French attitude may be attributed to a high degree to the influence of M. Jacques Léon Rueff. Whether in his capacity of theoretical economist or expert advisors of various French Governments, he used his influence for shaping French monetary policy in favour of strengthening the monetary use of gold not only in France but also in the international sphere. Thus after the *de facto* stabilisation of the franc in 1926, when the repatriation of French refugee funds enabled the Bank of France to accumulate a large foreign exchange reserve, he was on the side of those who favoured the conversion of a large proportion of foreign exchange holdings into gold. His attitude was inspired by his lifelong opposition to the gold exchange standard. Already in his comparatively subordinate capacity as Financial Attaché of the French Embassy in London he was able to influence the attitude of the Bank of France, of the French Finance Ministry and of

Poincaré himself, in a sense of pursuing a policy favouring the abandonment of the gold exchange standard and replacing it by the gold standard. Again during the 'sixties General de Gaulle and the French Finance Ministry followed M. Rueff's advice to pursue a policy against the gold exchange standard.

French statesmen and financial experts are essentially politically-minded. Their monetary policies ofter pursue political ends in the international sphere. The political motives that largely inspired the French crusade against the gold exchange standard in the late 'twenties were candidly disclosed in Émile Moreau's *Mémoires d'un Gouverneur de la Banque de France*. It contains extracts from Moreau's diary which he kept while Governor of the Bank of France during the two years which led to the legal stabilisation of the franc in 1928. It was edited for publication by M. Rueff – who contributed a preface to it – and it contains a mass of evidence indicating the essentially political motives of the French withdrawals of sterling balances during that period. This evidence irrefutably proves that, in addition to serving the financial objective of doing away with the gold exchange standard, the French policy served also the end of increasing France's political influence.

When history repeated itself in the middle 'sixties and France recovered her financial power as a result of the repatriation of French flight money after the termination of the Algiers troubles and their aftermaths, she was once more in a position to make herself felt in the international monetary sphere. She used her financial power for waging a 'Cold War' against the United States.

The Bank of France embarked on a crusade against the gold exchange standard by converting into gold most of its dollar holdings. Once more M. Rueff provided the theoretical background for the exercise and sought to justify not only the French withdrawals of gold but also the French efforts to persuade other Governments to act likewise. When France became the target of criticism for the political use of her financial power M. Rueff, in a broadcast interview, firmly denied any political motive of the gold withdrawals either on that occasion or even forty years earlier. He appeared to have forgotten that, by editing Moreau's *Mémoires* he himself supplied factual evidence on the political character of the French transactions in the late 'twenties.

On that occasion French financial power was used for ensuring French hegemony in Central and South-Eastern Europe. For instance, in an entry dated 27 January 1928, Moreau makes this crystal-clear:

'M. Rist [Deputy-Governor of the Bank of France] expressed his apprehension about the progress made by the Anglo-Yugoslav negotiations. Should the Bank of England deprive us from this client [the Yugoslav National Bank] to whose retention we attach importance for political reasons, I shall buy gold in London to indicate my displeasure.'

There are several passages of the same kind, but the above should suffice to remove any doubt about the essentially political nature of the French gold policy in 1928. By emphatically disclaiming the political motives behind the French gold operations of the late 'twenties M. Rueff cast doubts also on his disclaimer of the political motives behind the French gold operations of the late 'sixties. Human memory is short and the consequences of the French gold operations of 1926–28 might well have faded into oblivion if it had not been for the publication of Moreau's diary where the irrefutable evidence is given in cold print. Having edited the material for publication, M. Rueff's subsequent denial of facts freely admitted by Moreau carried but scant conviction.

On the more recent occasion the political aim of the French gold transaction was to weaken the United States financially, mainly in order to resist American economic penetration in Europe. While it was utterly unstatesmanlike and short-sighted on the part of General de Gaulle to try to reduce America's capacity to defend the free world in general and Western Europe in particular against the world-conquering ambitions of Soviet imperialism, there was undoubtedly a strong case for resisting American economic penetration, especially as it was financed largely with the aid of European money. France had also a good case in respect of her opposition to the creation of excessive international liquidity through the operation of the gold exchange standard. But the method chosen for making her policies prevail were anything but constructive. As the currency crises of the 'thirties were largely the consequences of French political misuse of financial power in the late 'twenties, the currency crises of the late 'sixties and early 'seventies were attributable to the repetition of history in the form of politically-motivated French financial transactions.

As I sought to make it plain in my book *The Destiny of the Dollar* and in various other writings, I was and still am against 'dollar-imperialism' in the form of the acquisition of European industries by American concerns at a time when the current balance of payments of the United States is strongly adverse. Even from an American point of view there is everything to be said against the toleration and encouragement of such transactions by the American authorities. To the extent to which they are financed with American money they add to the balance of payments deficit. To the extent to which they are financed abroad they prevent the United States from consolidating their external short-term liabilities by using their capacity to borrow from abroad for that purpose instead of for financing industrial expansion. The American balance of payments was affected unfavourably, for the exporting capacity of the American affiliates abroad came to compete with the exporting capacity of domestic American industries. Indeed these affiliates even exported a large proportion of their output to the American market, to the detriment of the current balance of payments. Their expansion was largely responsible for the increase of unemployment in the United States. If the idea of creating branch factories in Europe was prompted by the desire to keep down wages in the United States, that end was not achieved, judging by the escalation of American wage increases in 1969–72.

Aggressive American industrial penetration caused strong resentment not only in France but to a less extent also in other European countries. Even though General de Gaulle's

anti-American attitude was inspired in part by his petty urge
to retaliate for the slights he suffered at the hands of Roosevelt
during the war, the main cause was resentment over dollar-
imperialism. It consisted not only of industrial penetration
financed by European loans but also of the operation of the
system under which the United States had virtually a free hand
to overspend abroad on current account and on capital account
as the resulting balance of payments deficit was automatically
covered by the acquisition of dollars by the surplus countries.

General de Gaulle and M. Rueff were absolutely right in
opposing this system. But France could have dealt with it
without having to discredit the dollar in the process, by following Japan's example in banning American investment. Instead
she resorted to deliberate sabotage of the international monetary structure by trying her best to undermine confidence in
the dollar. At a time when the security and very existence of
the free nations depended on the American nuclear shield,
France under de Gaulle was doing her utmost to reduce
America's capacity to defend her and the rest of us.

Moreover, the open hostility of French policy tended to
antagonise American opinion and made it more difficult for
President Johnson and President Nixon to resist the isolationist
trend that was rearing its ugly head in the United States during
the late 'sixties and early 'seventies. Those of us who remember
how difficult it was in two World Wars to bring the United
States into the war on the side of Britain and France must
surely be aware of the utter folly of the irresponsible 'Yankee
go home' campaign. There is no such thing as gratitude in
politics, but even if France no longer remembers that the
United States helped to liberate her twice within a generation
she should bear in mind the possibility that American support
might be needed once more.

Mistakes have been made on both sides. There is no justi-
fication for the United States to take it for granted that she is
entitled to pursue policies at home and abroad which are bound
to result in a gigantic balance of payments deficit, on the
assumption that France and other countries absorb the resulting

dollar deficit as a matter of course. But there can be no excuse for the cold war atmosphere created by France in her attempts to frustrate American policies. It is to the interests of France as of the other free countries that the United States should be able to retain a strong strategic gold reserve without which she is bound to be handicapped in her effort to resist imperialist-Communist expansion.

Fortunately as a result of a personal meeting between President Nixon and President Pompidou in November 1971 Franco-American relationships improved and it was possible to arrange an agreed realignment of parities in December. But, while it was an important step to break the deadlock, there is still a long way from finding a solution which would restore the united front between the countries of the free world.

One of the causes of basic disagreement lies in the difference between the attitude of France and the United States towards the monetary role of gold. While between the two wars and also in the early post-war period there was a sharp contrast between the orthodox American attitude and the unwillingness or inability of France to pursue sound monetary policies, in more recent years it has been France that has come to represent financial conservatism and it has been the United States that has shown no willingness or ability to return to the straight and narrow path of sound finance. Ever since General de Gaulle has put the financial house of France in order she has become the champion of sound currency based on gold. At the same time the attitude of the United States has turned against gold and it is now the declared American policy to demonetise gold. France has strongly opposed such a change. And since judging by Mr Barber's statement at the IMF annual meeting in September 1971 Britain's attitude is inclined to conform to that of the United States, and even Germany has become converted in favour of a higher degree of flexibility of exchanges, France now remains the leading defender of sound monetary principles which had been championed by Britain and the United States in the past.

This situation carries the possibilities of a conflict, or at any rate a deplorable lack of unity. It also contains elements of rivalry. Towards the end of 1967 and early in 1968 France was in fact toying with the idea of making Paris the world financial centre. For years the franc had been firm in the vicinity of its maximum support point in relation to the dollar. It is possible that the removal of French exchange controls at the beginning of 1968 was intended to prepare the way for a bid for leadership in the sphere of international finance. The troubles in France in May and June 1968 brought about a severe setback and shattered these dreams. Indeed from being the strongest currency the franc became one of the weakest almost over night. It remained weak for some time and had to be devalued. In spite of this experience the idea of achieving leadership in the international monetary sphere – whether in isolation or as the senior partner in the enlarged EEC — has not been abandoned.

CHAPTER FOURTEEN

Gold and the Soviet Union

HAVING dealt with the attitude of one of the allied powers towards gold and the dollar, let us now examine the attitude of the potential aggressor – Soviet Russia. Owing to her large gold output she has become a factor of first-rate importance in the international gold situation.

No dependable statistics are available about the quantity of the gold output of the Soviet Union, but it is understood to be very substantial, and the potential gold resources of Siberia are known to be immense. Although Lenin originally favoured the demonetisation of gold – another instance of the sour-grapes complex, for the First World War and the Civil War depleted Russia's gold resources and reduced its gold output – Stalin came down strongly in favour of the monetary role of gold. The official textbook on economics which was passed for publication by Stalin himself shortly before his death emphasises that money must have intrinsic value and that gold is the most suitable material which confers intrinsic value on money.

Although gold production in the U.S.S.R. declined considerably during the Second World War – there was no need for gold between 1941 and 1945, for everything was imported under Lend-Lease – after the war considerable efforts were made to increase the gold output. Gold mining and alluvial gold production were given high priority, which meant that a high proportion of the limited quantity of modern equipment that was available or was imported was alloted to them. According to eye-witness accounts, some of the goldfields in the Soviet Union – notably those at Sverdlovsk – had a most up-to-date equipment, and the high quality of their manpower and management also indicated that the industry was given a high priority.

Up to the middle 'sixties a high proportion of the gold output was sold abroad in order to finance the import of much-needed capital equipment. In more recent years, however, the Soviet Government found it easy to obtain long-term credits abroad and also to borrow in the Euro-dollar market, so that the export of gold was no longer imperative. Between 1965 and 1971 there was little or no evidence of Soviet gold sales abroad, and since it is reasonable to assume that the output increased in all probability the Soviet Government or the State Bank of the USSR now possesses a substantial gold reserve.

Possibly the accumulation of a gold stock instead of its sale abroad is motivated by expectations of an increase of its price in terms of dollars and other exchanges. The Soviet Government shared the assumption held by hoarders of gold, that a substantial devaluation of the dollar could not be delayed for very long, and it considered it worth while to pay interest on foreign credits rather than use up its gold stock in payment for essential imports. A resumption of Soviet gold exports in June 1971 followed after the upward floating of the Deutschemark and of other currencies and of the revaluation of some of them. Until then a rise in the price of gold abroad must have been considered in Moscow to be a mere question of time. The revaluations and upwards floatings of 1971 drew attention, however, to the possibility that an increase in the dollar price of gold might be offset by a decline or reduction of its price in terms of other important currencies. In that case the Soviet Union might derive no net gain from deferring the sales of gold. More was said about the effect of devaluations and revaluations on the price of gold in *The Destiny of the Dollar*.

One of the reasons why the United States Government has been so reluctant to devalue the dollar and would prefer other Governments to revalue their currencies instead is precisely its unwillingness to assist the Soviet Union in obtaining a higher price for her exported gold. This is understandable. But those who think on such lines fail to realise that the Soviet Union stands to gain infinitely more from the disadvantages and handicaps the United States inflicts on herself by her unwillingness to devalue the dollar to a sufficient extent to ensure its stability and to obviate the necessity for credit restrictions, cuts in expenditure etc. in order to defend the dollar instead of devaluing it. So long as the dollar remains exposed to the risk of devaluation the United States cannot recover her old prestige and power. Too much effort has to be expended on the defence of the dollar and this reduces her capacity to assist other free nations threatened by Communist aggression.

Strangely enough it is widely believed in Washington that the defence of the dollar against a major devaluation – as distinct from its minor adjustments in 1971 – safeguards the prestige of the United States. Those who think on such lines forget that Germany and France suffered no permanent loss of financial prestige through the depreciation and devaluation of their currencies. Once the dollar is reduced to a level at which its maintenance presents no major problem it would recover its old prestige. The financial, economic, political and military gains derived from this would considerably outweigh the financial profits the Soviet Union would derive from a higher price obtained for her gold exports.

Another possible reason for the reluctance of the Soviet Union to export her gold output is the hope that the accumulation of a really substantial gold reserve would result in a considerable increase of her prestige. The rouble would be looked upon as a sound currency both within the Soviet Union and abroad. In Asia in particular the possession of a large gold reserve would increase the prestige of Soviet Russia, for most Asian peoples are very keen hoarders of precious metals. If at the same time the United States should try to demonetise gold completely, or that book entries would take the place of gold bars in Fort Knox and in the vaults of Federal Reserve Banks it would reduce her prestige considerably. The dollar would then be regarded as a second-rate currency compared with the rouble. The Soviet Union would be in a better position to finance a prolonged war abroad with the aid of her large gold reserve than the United States with the aid of large unused and unwanted SDRs.

It seems certain that even if the American price of gold should be raised so high that no further dollar devaluations could reasonably be expected the Soviet Union would retain a very considerable part of her gold reserve and would do her utmost to increase it through a further increase of her gold output in Siberia and elsewhere. Gold would only be exported to pay for urgently needed goods which could not be imported against long term credits. In any case the Kremlin is no doubt aware of the advantages of owing the largest possible amounts of debts to the free world. Any repudiation of this debt might trigger off a major crisis in the West, especially if it is well timed and if the United States and other Western countries relinquish the benefits of possessing large gold stocks as a security reserve against crises.

From an American point of view it would be highly advantageous if the price of gold were raised sufficiently to enable the United States to repay her external short-term liabilities out of her gold reserve. The fact that the United States is once more able to do so would inspire confidence in the dollar and holders of dollars would not want to convert their holdings. The financial and political advantage of such a change in the situation would heavily outweigh the financial and political advantages derived by the Soviet Union from a few additional billions of dollars she would receive for her gold exports.

Since the gold output in Soviet Russia does not depend on the profits determined by the price of gold it would be unaffected by a major devaluation of the dollar. As already pointed out, the Soviet Government aims at building up an impressive gold reserve. This would increase its financial and political prestige and power and would be therefore to the detriment of the free world. But the leading Western countries have the remedy in their own hands. All they would have to do would be to stop granting loans and credits to Soviet Russia so long as she pursues her present aggressive imperialist policy aiming at world conquest. It is extremely short-sighted on the part of the

Western nations to assist the Soviet Union to increase its productive capacity with the aid of imported equipment financed with borrowed money. It recalls the £1,000 m. loan offer made by the Chamberlain Government to Hitler in 1939, with the difference that tomorrow's aggressor has not refused the loan.

A further increase of Soviet debts to Western countries would increase the temptation to default on the debts. It must be borne in mind that, even though up to now the Soviet Union has met her external liabilities she has done so as a matter of expediency rather than as a matter of commercial integrity. The moment it would become expedient for financial or political reasons to default she would undoubtedly do so without hesitation.

But apart altogether from this consideration, foreign credits help the Soviet Union to build up a powerful gold reserve. In the absence of such credits she would have to choose between reducing her gold reserve by selling more gold abroad or diverting more of her producing capacity to gold production, to the detriment of the expansion of her industrial and military power. This consideration is much more important from the point of view of the freedom and security of the Western world than the advantage of the higher price that the Soviet Government would receive for her gold exports after a major devaluation of the dollar. It would be an ill-timed as well as ill-advised move on the part of the United States to demote the dollar to the rank of a perpetually inconvertible second-rate paper currency at the time when the Soviet Union is making a supreme effort to raise the rouble to the rank of a gold-backed currency.

CHAPTER FIFTEEN

The 'Sour-Grapes Complex'

IT is one of the absurdities of monetary history that the United
States of all countries, the holder of the largest gold reserve ever
since the First World War, and a gold producer, should lead
the anti-gold crusade. It is true, the American gold reserve has
declined from some $25 billion to somewhat below $10 billion.
Even so, at the time of writing it is still larger than the gold
reserve of any other country. If, as American and other anti-
gold crusaders believe, a de-monetisation of gold would greatly
reduce its value, then it would be against the interests of the
United States as a holder of gold and one of the producers of
gold, to agitate for its de-monetisation. Quite on the contrary,
it would be in accordance with American interests from that
point of view to favour a substantial increase in the price of
gold.

Although Britain's holding of gold is smaller than that of
several other leading countries, it is far from negligible. Besides,
a high proportion of South African and other gold mining
shares is owned in the UK. Why then is it, it may well be asked,
that the United States and Britain should lead the movement
aiming at a de-monetisation of gold? A possible answer is that
neither country has a sufficiently large gold reserve left to meet
their increased monetary requirements, and since they are
unable to replenish their reserves to a sufficient extent they have
developed a 'sour grapes complex.' They have not enough gold
and are unable to get enough gold, so they emulate Aesop's fox
who, having been unable to reach the grapes he wanted badly,
comforted himself by pretending that anyhow the grapes were
too sour. Neither his pretence, nor that of the Americans or

British authorities about gold, really convinced anyone, not even their good selves.

Until recently both countries were the leading champions of monetary stability in terms of gold. Having suffered much inconvenience during the post-war period through the rigidity of their gold parities, they have now worked up an enthusiastic support for the idea of discarding that system, so as to be able to devalue cheerfully each time the maintenance of their parties would necessitate the adoption of unpleasant measures, and whenever the defence of their gold parities tends to prevent them from increasing or at any rate maintaining their rate of growth. This change of attitude is yet another manifestation of the debasement of the Anglo-Saxon character. Taking the line of least resistance is not the attitude that had built the British Empire and had raised the United States to the rank of the leading world power.

Neither Government could possibly be really enthusiastic about having to dispose of their gold stocks at a loss. And they could not possibly be indifferent about heavy losses by investors in both countries who hold large amounts of gold mining shares. But evidently the British and American Governments are prepared to face these losses for the sake of securing their freedom to inflate and to devalue. They expect it to bring political advantages to the Conservative Party in Britain and to the Republican Party in the United States to remove one of the remaining obstacles to a magnanimous distribution of bribes to their respective electorates, without having to make their taxpayers pay the cost. It could be paid by means of stepping up inflation. The cost of inflation would not be realised by the public until it has reached an advanced stage. What does not seem to occur to Tories or to Republicans is that the Labour Party in Britain and the Democrats in the United States could also play the same game, and that they might play it even better than their political opponents, judging by Britain's experience under the Wilson Government and America's experience under the Roosevelt Administration. The elimination of gold discipline – what is left of it – from the monetary system would step up competitive wholesale bribery of the electorates in both countries. It would escalate inflation.

Another reason for the United States to favour the removal of gold from the monetary system is that South Africa and the Soviet Union are the main gold-producing countries. South Africa is unpopular in the United States because of apartheid. But it is difficult to imagine how the African mine workers – whether white or black or coloured – and those who depend on their earnings directly or indirectly would stand to benefit by the sharp decline in gold mining which the anti-gold school expects to be the result of a de-monetisation of gold. As for Britain, a slump in the value of her large holdings of gold mining shares would be a major disaster, the effects of which would not be confined by any means to investors.

On the face of it there appears to be a stronger case for inflicting a blow at the Soviet Union by reducing the potential value of her gold exports through a de-monetisation of gold. The same arguments which are used against an increase in the price of gold – dealt with in Chapter 14 and in my book *The Destiny of the Dollar* – are applied by the anti-gold school also in favour of a de-monetisation gold. Beyond doubt, on the face of it it would be a blow to the Soviet Government which has given a high priority to gold mining and has accumulated a very large gold stock in the hope of being able to obtain for its gold exports a higher price after a major devaluation of the dollar. But from a politico-military point of view it would suit the interests of the Communist camp if the United States were to deprive itself of a substantial reserve which had the advantage of being always acceptable abroad in time of war as well as in time of peace.

The traditional argument of those who want to terminate the monetary use of gold is that it is wrong to make the volume of credit available for financing economic growth dependent on the caprices of nature. This argument may have carried some conviction under the pure gold standard. But it was of very limited validity under the managed gold standard, under the gold exchange standard or under the Bretton Woods system.

It would cease altogether to be valid if and when the Barber Plan for the extended use of SDRs should become fully operative. The application of that plan would of course greatly reduce the relative importance of gold in the monetary system, importance which was already gradually reduced with the gradual departure from the pure gold standard and with the resulting decline of the proportion of gold in official reserves. But it is one thing to reduce the proportion of gold held in total Central Bank reserves and quite a different thing to pursue a deliberate declared policy aiming at completely terminating the monetary role of gold.

The most likely explanation of the American-British attitude is that the authors and supporters of the SDR scheme are afraid that, so long as gold continues to play some monetary role, by its mere existence it challenges comparison with SDRs and with inconvertible paper currencies which would represent the bulk of the Central Banks' reserves under the system outlined by Mr Barber. The comparison between gold with a substantial intrinsic value and book entries representing claims which may or may not be accepted in payment by surplus countries would be distinctly to the disadvantage of the latter. For this reason any Central Bank with a modicum of common sense would naturally aim at maintaining the highest possible proportion of their reserves in the form of gold. From the point of view of the SDR scheme it might appear, therefore, on the face of it an advantage if gold could be demonetised altogether so as to eliminate a preferable alternative device.

Before gold became the principal monetary object all sorts of objects, many of them with no intrinsic value, were used for monetary purposes. On the face of it it might, therefore, sound reasonable to suppose, that, if only gold could cease to be considered a monetary metal, book entries with no intrinsic value might come to be considered as money, for want of better. Governments are in a position to exclude gold from their reserves or from those of their Central Banks, in the same way as they had excluded silver.

It would be easy to pass legislation compelling Central Banks to cease to use gold for monetary purposes. It would be quite another story to try to persuade the public to follow their example. If Central Banks wanted to rid themselves of their gold reserves all they would have to do would be to restore the free convertibility of their notes for the benefit of private holders. Their gold stocks, or those of their Governments, would disappear into private hoards in a very short time, and coins and bars would then remain in private circulation. In particular whenever there appears to be the possibility of a war, or of civil disorder, or of bank failure, the popularity of officially demonetised gold would soar in the private sector, and so would its price in terms of the official paper currency.

The support given by many theoretical economists to the idea of demonetising gold is largely due to the prevailing growth-hysteria. Expansion and still more expansion at all costs has become the favourite slogan. According to the popular view, the monetary use of gold is an obstacle to accelerated expansion which must be eliminated. Moreover, since there is a risk that its continued existence as part of the Central Banks' reserve might handicap the unlimited increase in the volume of paper credit, co-existence of gold with paper credit must end. Anything that slows down the pace of growth is considered anti-social, on the grounds that it keeps down the standard of living and prevents mankind from making use of technological progress. But there is another side to the picture.

As we saw in Chapter 10, this ideology has been challenged recently by a school of thought which is gravely concerned by pollution, by the deterioration of the environment, by the wastage of irreplaceable resources and by increased consumption resulting from the rapid growth of world population and its rising standard of living. Of course, expansionists denounce them as scaremongers. Yet it is impossible to open a newspaper without coming across flagrant instances that confirm their fears. Rising standard of living is accompanied by increasing pollution and wastage. Egalitarianism accentuates that trend, for it steps up the consumption and production of all kinds of goods, especially of consumer durables. Even nature is tampered with through the employment of artificial methods to increase the agricultural output at the cost of more pollution as a result of spraying with noxious chemicals.

All this deterioration of the environment is liable to become escalated if, as seems probable, the last remains of the discipline imposed on the economy by the limited monetary use of gold are eliminated. Inflationary expansion will then gather momentum, with all its damaging economic and environmental effects. If the monetary use of gold did no more than slow down the 'progress' of mankind towards self-destruction it would amply justify itself.

There is, of course, everything to be said for an increase in the standard of living. But it must be a planned process and those planning it must pay due regard to environmental considerations.

CHAPTER SIXTEEN

Proposed Substitutes for Gold

THE perpetual scarcity of gold – that is, the excess of monetary requirements over its supply – has been a problem throughout the ages. In the earlier periods innumerable Governments sought to solve it through the debasement of the coinage and private individuals followed their example. Alchemists tried to invent a method of producing gold artificially, without any success. European monetary experts from John Law onward – and long before him Governments in China – were more successful in inducing the public to accept paper money as a substitute for gold. In early instances, and also in some more recent instances, these gold substitutes came to be discredited in due course, not because they had no intrinsic value but because the possibility of their production in unlimited quantities removed the necessary discipline which the monetary use of gold imposes on the economy. If the quantity of printed pieces of paper or of book entries representing money could be kept down in the same way as nature keeps down the quantity of gold they would be almost as suitable as gold for serving as money.

But far too many Governments are not sufficiently strong-minded to resist the temptation to solve their financial problems by resorting to the proverbial stroke of the pen which increases the amount of fictitious means of payment at their disposal. And the main reason why some Governments have turned recently against gold is that its quantity has its inconvenient natural limitations and its very existence tends to discredit the gold substitutes that can be multiplied at will.

Other Governments want to get away from gold as a standard

of value because such use of gold makes it more difficult for them to devalue whenever it suits them. When putting forward his SDR plan, Mr Barber stated with a disarming candour that the use of SDRs instead of gold would relieve the Governments of their inhibition that made it more difficult for them under the Bretton Woods system to devalue.

Paper money itself was originally meant to be simply a gold substitute. For a long time its quantity was supposed to be kept down to the amount of gold cover held against it. The notes were supposed to be simply receipts for gold deposited with dependable depositaries – goldsmiths in the early days and later banks. It was distinctly advantageous to use this gold substitute for circulation – always provided that its recipients and holders could be certain that its full gold counterpart was really in safe keeping at the depositaries.

In due course it was discovered that all holders of these gold substitutes never presented their notes for redemption at the same time, so that the depositaries were reasonably safe to lend a certain proportion of the gold deposits, or to issue notes in addition to the amount of the deposits they held, on the assumption that their holdings of gold were sufficient to meet withdrawals. On many occasions they miscalculated, however, and they were unable to redeem all their notes when owing to some crisis there was a run of depositors.

At a further stage the inconvertibility of paper notes came to be openly recognised by official issuing institutions and the value of the gold substitutes was upheld by a limitation of their quantity and by the future prospects of convertibility. Today there are hardly any more notes in circulation which are really convertible into gold. The text of the notes still contain promises to that effect, but they are obviously meaningless and nobody takes them seriously. The promise made by the Chief Cashier of the Bank of England on behalf of the Governor and Company of his bank, 'I Promise to pay the bearer on Demand the sum of One Pound' or 'Five Pounds' or 'Ten Pounds,' are a standing joke. Everybody knows that, should holders of the notes present them at the Bank's counters in the expectation that this solemn promise would be honoured, the Chief Cashier could do no more than exchange them for notes of equal value, which would be a pointless time-wasting exercise.

The statutory limitation of the quantity of notes no longer safeguards their value in terms of goods, because the volume of money and credit has come to be adapted in practice to expanding requirements. This is why the monetarists school is utterly devoid of realities in contending that the economy can be managed by regulating the quantity of money. In prevailing circumstances that quantity is not the cause but the effect. It is made to conform to the requirements of the economy, requirements which again are determined by the degree of wage and price inflation and that of economic growth. It has become politically and socially impossible to keep down the quantity of money if inadequacy of its supply causes an increase of unemployment or prevents economic growth at a politically acceptable rate.

Hence the tendency to reject the discipline imposed on the economy by the monetary role of gold. Even though the handicap it represents can be mitigated by the adoption of the managed gold standard, or the gold exchange standard, or the Bretton Woods system, this is not enough for those who suffer from growth-hysteria. They are just as anxious to remove balance of payments discipline as they are to remove gold discipline. If the weakening of the gold discipline leads to inflation which in turn causes a balance of payments deficit it comes to be considered essential to adopt gold substitutes – such as SDRs – that obviate the necessity for a deficit country to work harder or to consume less.

Of course the gold exchange standard and the Bretton Woods system has gone a long way towards applying substitutes for gold as a means for covering international deficits. A further step was taken in that direction by the adoption of the device of Special Drawing Rights – to supplement the increasing amount of ordinary drawing rights available under the original rules of the IMF – and of reciprocal swap facilities arranged between Central Banks. The difference between these various types of facilities and SDRs is that the former devices only provide temporary facilities which are repayable by the borrower in due course, while 70 per cent of the SDR is a free gift to beneficiaries. The Barber Plan enunciated in 1971 goes even further. He proposed to do away with the credit element in SDRs. Under his scheme all SDRs, whether already issued under the Rio de Janeiro scheme or to be issued after the new plan comes to be applied, are to become free gifts pure and simple. No obligation whatsoever of repayment will be attached to them. They will become manna dropped from the sky and picked up by the recipients – or to mention a more recent instance, they will constitute free bonuses similar to those paid out under the social credit system applied in Alberta.

Gold has to be mined at a considerable cost and its production is discouraged if the cost of production in lower-grade ore mines rises above its value. The cost of production of SDRs will consist of the cost of the ledgers into which they are entered, of the clerical labour of entering them and transferring them and of postal or telegraphic charges. Its sum total is so negligible that the increase of its quantity encounters no obstacle whatsoever on that ground. Such self-restraint as the issuing authorities are capable of practising will be the only limiting influence. A limit of $9.5 billion was fixed for the original issue of SDRs. It remains to be seen what maximum limit, if any, will be fixed for the proposed new issue. According to the Barber Plan its limit is to be determined by the growing current requirements of mankind, plus the amount of dollar and sterling balances to be converted into SDRs.

Under the gold standard the requirements of mankind were liable to be left unsatisfied owing to an inadequacy of gold supplies to meet them. The system has often been criticised on the ground that the financial resources available to mankind depend on the 'caprices of nature.' If gold were freely available and its output could be determined by Government policy Governments and economists would not object to its monetary role. Since, however, the quantity of gold cannot be increased at will Governments which have not enough of it have come to emulate Aesop's fox by pretending that it is not really suitable for monetary purposes.

It is also considered inconvenient to depend for supplementing international liquid resources on the adverse balance of payments of other countries. As I tried to explain in *The Destiny of the Dollar*, the conception under which balance of payments deficits are considered international liquid resources is utterly fallacious. International liquidity is required for the purpose of covering balance of payments deficits. It is therefore needed by the deficit countries themselves and not by the surplus countries. So to those who object to depending on balance of payments deficits on the ground that they do not necessarily arise in accordance with requirements the answer is that dependence on balance of payments deficits for liquid reserves is an absurdity. The trouble is not that countries do not necessarily unbalance their balance of payments whenever other countries need a surplus but that it is deficit countries and not surplus countries that need liquid resources for international purposes.

Of course international liquid reserves serve not only the purpose of meeting balance of payments deficits but also the purpose of facilitating the financing of domestic economic expansion. Both surplus countries and deficit countries welcome therefore the additions to their liquid reserves in the form of new issues of SDRs. On the assumption that expansion is in all circumstances a Good Thing the invention of SDRs and the projected extension of their use is naturally very popular. If only Governments and Central Banks could be induced to accept SDRs. This explains the keenness of many surplus countries to have even bigger surpluses. In addition to improving their balance of payments and increasing their international reserves, the deficits of other countries help them to finance accelerated growth at home. Even though in most countries the volume of domestic credit is no longer related to the size of their international reserves, they do have to restrain credit if those reserves decline to danger level, and they feel at liberty to expand credit if thanks to the deficits of other countries they are able to build up a comfortable surplus of reserves above immediate requirements. It is no wonder, therefore, that Western European Governments viewed with concern any effort of the United States to reduce her trade deficit. It is difficult, however, to persuade a deficit country to abstain from trying to work out its salvation and remain in deficit just for the sake of obliging the surplus countries.

It is difficult to reconcile the conflict of interests between deficit countries and surplus countries. One of the reasons why the idea that SDRs should take the place of trade deficits as a device to supplement liquid resources has been so popular is that they are capable of adding to the liquid resources of both surplus countries and deficit countries. The surplus countries' meat need not be the deficit countries' poison.

If Governments and Central Banks could be induced to accept SDRs in unlimited amounts it would enable deficit countries to abstain from putting their houses in order for the sake of balancing their international accounts. One of the reasons why monetary authorities are not likely to accept unlimited amounts of SDRs is that there exist liquid assets which are preferable to SDRs because they are accepted by all surplus countries in unlimited amounts. So to ensure the popularity of SDRs as reserve assets it would seem to be convenient to terminate the monetary use of gold. This is very understandable. But gold could not be wished out of existence.

CHAPTER SEVENTEEN

The Limitations of 'Paper-Gold'

IT is understandable that Governments and Central Banks should be in favour of supplementing their international liquid reserves by some assets which would enable them to permit the economies of their respective countries to expand with comparative impunity – that is with a reduced risk of 'punishment' in the form of a fall of their reserves below safety level. It is equally understandable that they would like this reserve asset to be expandable at will – or at any rate at the collective will of a group of leading Governments. They are unable to bring about at will an increase in the world's gold output or the world's monetary supply of gold – except through an increase in the official price of gold, a solution which is apt to encounter strong opposition – and they are unable to compel Governments of other countries to oblige them by increasing international liquidity through maintaining a big balance of payments deficit. Nor can surplus countries be persuaded to hold the currencies of deficit countries in unlimited amounts.

On the other hand there was no difficulty in increasing the resources of the IMF through the increase of total quotas, in stages, from their original level of 1946. To these resources the $6 billion arranged under the General Agreement to Borrow, many more billions of reciprocal swap arrangements between Central Banks, and the allocation of $9.5 billion under the original Rio de Janeiro agreement were added.

As a result of all these arrangements the proportion of monetary gold reserves to total Central Bank reserves declined considerably. Even so, it is still at an appreciable level. It is the intention of the Governments who agreed to the basic principles of the Barber Plan providing for the creation of unlimited amounts of a new type of non-redeemable Special Drawing Rights to reduce further the proportion of gold to total reserves through the increase of the proportion of SDRs. This is understandable. What is more difficult to understand is their ambition to demonetise gold altogether and replace it almost entirely by SDRs.

Why should it be preferable to hold SDRs as international liquid reserves *instead of gold*? The desire to hold them *in addition to their gold* is understandable. But why should any Government or Central Bank find it more advantageous to rely on fictitious book entries rather than on solid gold in their vaults or earmarked in the vaults of other Central Banks or of an international institution? If the irredeemable claims represented by these book entries should really fulfil all expectations of their advocate they might become as acceptable as gold for meeting international balance of payments deficits. But it is difficult to imagine any situation in which these book entries would become *more* acceptable internationally than gold.

Enthusiastic advocates of the scheme providing for the issue of non-repayable SDRs are naturally keen on discrediting gold as a medium in which to settle balance of payments deficits, so as to make the holding of SDRs more attractive. The fact that some Governments and Central Banks profess themselves to be prepared to face heavy losses on their demonetised gold stocks for the sake of ensuring the acceptability of SDRs gives some idea of their intentions about the magnitude of the issues of SDRs they have in mind. If they should be able to add many billions of SDRs to their reserves as free gifts which would never be repayable it is understandable that they should be prepared to shoulder losses running into hundreds of millions or even billions as a result of a depreciation of their gold reserves to the value which they would retain because of their non-monetary use. The fact that the Barber Plan and subsequent statements made by President Nixon and Mr Connally stressed the need for a demonetisation of gold can only be interpreted as an indication of the intention to issue tens of billions of dollars of SDRs. For it would not be worth while to face the loss on the gold stocks of Britain and the United States, and on their investments in the gold mining industry, for the sake of their quotas out of an issue of, say, another $9.5 billion. To make the sacrifice worth while the gifts of SDRs they intend to allocate to themselves must be surely well in excess of their losses.

The fact that the two leading countries advocating SDRs want to adopt the new reserve assets not in addition to their gold stocks but instead of them clearly shows their intention to misuse that device through over-issuing SDRs. In the first instance they want to use SDRs for the 'repayment' of the excessive sterling and dollar balances held by other monetary authorities and possibly also much of the sterling and dollar balances held by unofficial holders. It seems they consider it well worth their while to write off losses on their gold reserves for the sake of ridding themselves of the millstones round their necks represented by these external short-term liabilities. In theory only official holdings of dollar and sterling balances would be 'consolidated' by their conversion into SDRs. In practice privately held dollar or sterling balances can, and do, find their way into the Central Banks reserves whenever private holders develop a distrust in the dollar or sterling. So the grand total which might be converted into SDRs might well assume very considerable dimensions.

It is clearly understood that neither the IMF nor any Central Bank or Government is responsible for the conversion or redemption of SDRs to any participants in the scheme. From this point of view it is an even less satisfactory reserve currency than the dollar which could always be sold at a price or could be spent on American exports. In theory, the gold value of SDRs is supposed to be guaranteed, but since nobody is responsible for their repayment the guarantee of the rate at which they are supposed to be repaid is of a problematic value. Admittedly, holders can always call upon the IMF to order another participant Government to convert their SDRs into its own currency or into some other convertible currency. But since all participants are in a position to contract out of the scheme at a moment's notice, this rule might well become unenforceable, for situations are liable to arise in which participants might prefer to contract out of the scheme rather than increase their holdings of SDRs.

Everything depends on the total of outstanding SDRs and their distribution among participants. If too large amounts are allotted for the 'consolidation' of dollar and sterling balances and for covering the gigantic current American balance of payments deficits a stage might easily be reached when no Government would be willing to accept any more SDRs in settlement of its country's balance of payments surpluses. This situation was discussed in some detail in my book *The Destiny of the Dollar*. Here we are mainly concerned with the defects of the SDR scheme from the point of view of its impact on the future of gold. What was said above is more than sufficient to reinforce the contention of the present book that most Governments and Central Banks will always prefer gold to SDRs.

There is much to be said for supplementing the gold reserves and foreign exchange reserves of Central Banks and Governments by allocation of SDRs, always provided that the rate of their allocation is moderate. It would be considerably to the advantage of the United States and of the free world in general if the millstone of the American external floating debt could be removed through its consolidation in some form. This consideration is of course of first-rate importance. But if such a consolidation should encourage the Nixon Administration to continue pursuing the irresponsible policy it has been pursuing for the sake of winning the election it would do the United States much more harm than good in the long run.

This is the main reason why political considerations must not be allowed to override our misgivings about the risk of SDR inflation. Important as it is to relieve the United States of the burden of her gigantic external short-time indebtedness for the sake of restoring her financial powers and prestige, if this end is sought to be achieved at the cost of a further weakening of the American character the price would be grossly excessive. Apart from other considerations, the much-desired end could not be achieved except quite temporarily. In the absence of a supreme effort on the part of the American people to work out its own salvation the reduction of its external indebtedness would be a short-lived achievement. The restoration of the prestige of the dollar by converting official dollar balances into SDRs would provide irresistible temptation and ample opportunity for the United States to contract fresh external short-term debts, so that before very long foreign holdings of dollar balances would be just as big as they were before their reduction with the aid of the SDR allocations.

It would be infinitely preferable to retain some degree os discipline by means of stipulating that the allocation of SDRl must be subject to reserve requirements, just as the additionaf General Drawing Rights are. A certain percentage of the SDRs should be covered by a gold reserve to be held by IMF. This would inspire more confidence in SDRs and would also keep their quantity under some degree of control.

Those who would object to such provisions ought to be reminded that in any case the issue of SDRs would have its natural limitations. The absence of gold from the monetary system would not induce Central Banks of surplus countries to accept SDRs in unlimited amounts, so that their excessive issue would entail the risk of a collapse of the system.

Fortunately, 'consolidation' of the excessive foreign holdings of dollar balances by means of over-issuing SDRs is not the only possible solution of the problem. The real burden of those balances in terms of gold or goods and services could and should be reduced by means of a substantial devaluation of the dollar. This problem will be examined in the next two chapters.

CHAPTER EIGHTEEN

The Case for a Higher Price of Gold

THE error of judgement of those advocates of the new SDR scheme who wanted SDRs to replace gold altogether was already pointed out in Chapters 16 and 17. Owing to the gravity of the error and of its possible consequences it is necessary, however, to go into one aspect of this subject in greater detail. The main arguments in favour of substantial additional issues of SDRs are that it makes the volume of international liquidity independent of the volume of monetary gold or of balance of payments deficits of countries with reserve currencies and that it relieves the United States and Britain of the burden of excessive foreign balances through consolidating them. The dangers of a further spectacular increase in the volume of unsecured non-self-liquidating credits have already been dealt with in earlier chapters. This inverted pyramid would rest on much more solid foundations if it were based on gold reserves the size of which would bear a reasonable ratio to the volume of credit. That end could not possibily be achieved on the basis of a gold price of $38 or even of the basis of the market price of gold at the time of writing, which is some fifteen dollars higher.

The price of gold was kept down artificially at $35 between 1934 and 1971 and its increase by a mere 8½ per cent was quite unrealistic. Prices, the cost of production and cost of living have increased at least fourfold since before the war, and it would be reasonable to adapt the price of gold to the general level of prices by raising it to about $140. This would create an adequate gold backing for the expanded volume of credit and the resulting de-hoarding and increased output would provide adequate backing for any reasonable future credit expansion for constructive purposes.

Above all, a 75 per cent devaluation of the dollar would enable the United States to restore convertibility of official dollar holdings. As I tried to argue in *The Destiny of the Dollar*, it is of the utmost importance to restore the financial power and prestige of the United States for the sake of enabling her to continue to fulfil her role as the principal defender of the free world. This consideration must transcend any other consideration, economic or political. It is even more important than the defence of the environment, for every self-respecting person would prefer even to live in a polluted world than to live under Communist dictatorship.

Of course it may be argued by advocates of the SDR scheme that the same end could be achieved through the conversion of surplus dollar balances into SDRs. But, as I tried to explain in Chapter 17, it is doubtful whether the world's absorbing capacity for SDRs is sufficient to allow for such a major exercise. If it were spread over a period of years it would mean a prolongation of the uncertainty that exists at the time of writing. Unless an early solution is found the sword of Damocles of a disastrous crisis would continue to hang over our heads. We cannot afford to delay the restoration of a stable and dependable system.

For this reason it is absolutely essential that the consolidation of surplus dollar balances should take place in the not too distant future, simultaneously with a major devaluation of the dollar and the restoration of its convertibility. If large amounts of SDRs are issued – as they have to be if they are used for consolidating the external floating indebtedness of the United States as well as for financing economic growth – they should not be mere fictitious book-entries as they are intended to be under the Barber Plan. They should have a substantial proportion of gold cover to ensure their convertibility. And so long as the price of gold is at its present level the required quantity of gold is just not available. Whether SDRs will become an additional source of potential danger or an additional source

of creative liquid reserves depends on whether the price of
gold is raised sufficiently to make it practicable to base SDR
allocations on adequate gold backing. It may be a matter of
argument whether the reserve ratio should be 25 per cent or
33 per cent or 40 per cent. But it is beyond doubt that in the
absence of a confidence-inspiring gold backing for SDRs a
crise de confiance that would wreck the SDR system would be a
mere question of time.

Another reason why it is imperative to raise the price of gold
substantially with one stroke lies in the disadvantages of mini-
devaluations. France had ample experience in this sphere both
in the late 'thirties and after the war. Mini-devaluations just
don't inspire any confidence and their psychological effect is
therefore wasted. This conclusion is confirmed by the American
experience of 1971–72. Most experts agree that the realignment
of parities on 18 December 1971 more or less removed the
disequilibrium between currencies, so that the dollar was
no longer overvalued. Nevertheless in a matter of two months
the dollar was the subject of a sweeping speculative attack.
Even before Congress passed its devaluation to $38 per ounce
of gold a second mini-devaluation came to be widely anticipated. Alternatively it was expected that the support given by
foreign Central Banks would be discontinued owing to their
unwillingness to increase further their holdings of unwanted
dollars, and then the dollar would resume its downward
floating.

This experience went a long way towards confirming my
conclusion in my *Destiny of the Dollar* – passed for press prior to
the dollar crises that developed during the early months of 1972
– that there must be a maxi-devaluation, not a mini-devaluation.
Apart altogether from the need for restoring the capacity of the
United States to convert into gold official dollar holdings, and
from the need of raising the amount of monetary gold sufficiently high to provide partial but adequate cover to the principal
currencies as well as to SDRs, the devaluation must be sufficient
to make it appear unlikely that another and yet another
devaluation would follow. It must appear to be 'a devaluation

to end devaluations' at any rate for a long time to come. This
is the only way in which confidence in the dollar and in the
stability of the international currency system could be restored.

Needless to say, a major devaluation of the dollar could not
take place in isolation. Other currencies would follow it, either
as a result of an agreed realignment similar to the one arranged
on 18 December 1971, only on a more realistic basis, or as a
result of the adaptation of other currencies to the dollar. Needless to say, a devaluation race would create chaotic conditions
so that an agreed realignment would be indefinitely preferable.
But even if this should prove to be impossible it seems reasonable to hope that most Governments would not wish either to
be left behind with grossly overvalued currencies or to try to
outbid the United States in respect of the content of their
devaluations and frustrate the latter's effort to solve the problem of the dollar which is the problem of the entire free
world.

If all the maxi-devaluations were to take place more or less
simultaneously there is no reason why price levels in the United
States and other countries should be affected by the act of the
devaluations. If the Governments concerned should misuse the
increased liquidity represented by the higher bookkeeping
value of their gold reserves then of course the country concerned
would take the consequences. But if a large part of the increased
amount of gold reserves should be used for providing SDRs
with a gold backing and increasing the proportion of gold in
monetary reserves, an inflationary use of the larger monetary
gold stocks would not follow their increase as a matter of
course.

The political argument against a major increase in the price
of gold is that it would strengthen the wealth and power of the
Soviet Union. Since the problem of Soviet Imperialism is
highly important we dealt with it in detail in Chapter 14.
A higher gold price would of course increase the purchasing
power of the Soviet Union abroad. But this could be offset by
discontinuing the granting of credits to the Soviet Union.
Instead of importing in a credit basis Soviet Russia would pay

by selling gold abroad, thereby further strengthening the reserves backing SDRs and the principal currencies.

Admittedly the increase of the financial resources of the Soviet Union as a result of the higher price of gold would also increase its political power. But this would be offset by the effect of an increase of Siberian gold output on Sino-Soviet relations. Even as it is those relations are far from being ideal from the point of view of Communist imperialism. But given the fact that gold means a great deal to China as indeed to all Eastern races, the possibility of securing the possession of the Siberian goldfields would greatly increase the influence of those Chinese political leaders who are hostile to Moscow. The main reason why the hawks of the Kremlin have abstained from taking advantage of the superior military power achieved by Soviet Russia in the early 'seventies for conquering Western Europe, the Middle East or India lies in their fear that they might find themselves confronted not only with the West and with Japan but also with China. Possibly they hope that with the death or retirement of Mao Tse-tung the political constellation in Peking might change in their favour. But the temptation to become the second largest, or possibly the largest gold producer in the world is liable to influence Chinese opinion in favour of pursuing the end of liberating Siberia from Russian colonialism. The higher the value of gold is raised the stronger this consideration is likely to weigh in determining whether China will be an ally or an enemy to Soviet Russia.

Once it is recognised that the United States and the rest of the free world would stand to benefit greatly by a higher gold price it would be a puerile attitude to oppose it on the ground that a country whose method of government is disliked would also stand to benefit by it. The trouble is that while the profit derived by Soviet Russia from the higher price of gold is direct and obvious, the profit derived from it by the United States is a matter of controversy. There are arguments on both sides, and public opinion is bound to be divided about the relative advantages and disadvantages. Economists for and against a major increase in the official dollar price of gold are apt to argue each other to a standstill, so that politicians cannot get a clear guidance. No public pressure in favour of a major devaluation is likely to develop, and it will be difficult for those in favour of a higher price of gold to persuade the Administration that they have an unanswerable case.

CHAPTER NINETEEN

Prospects of Gold

THE last chapter stated the case for a substantial rise in the
price of gold. The question we now have to examine is, what
are the prospects for a much-needed substantial rise in the
price of gold? It would be sheer wishful thinking to expect
it to materialise at any rate during the next few years. The
need for it has not been realised sufficiently widely in American official circles or by the American public, and the idea
encounters strong opposition.

It goes without saying that those who are in favour of a de-
monetisation of gold are firmly against its further appreciation,
though even such a fanatical opponent of the monetary role of
gold as Mr Connally had to concede a minor increase of its
official price, and thanks to his policies its free market price
rose quite considerably. Anti-gold agitation is no longer
confined to a handful of currency cranks of the type of the
social credit school. The idea to eliminate gold has now
adherents in many respectable quarters – indeed in some quite
unexpected quarters. I had to argue against the de-monetisation
of gold on the premises of a Central Bank which had been the
shrine of the worship of the golden calf. An old-established firm
of bullion brokers is quite openly against a rise in the price of
gold and misses few opportunities for forecasting its fall. On one
occasion I even had a heated argument defending the *raison
d'être* of gold in the very room where its London market price
is fixed twice a day, beholding ashtrays full of cigarette ends
deposited there by representatives of all bullion firms a few
minutes earlier in the course of the fixing.

But while those in favour of a de-monetisation of gold are

naturally against a rise of its price, this does not mean that those against its de-monetisation are necessarily in favour of its rise. Nor does it mean that those agitating for the rise of its price and for an increase of its monetary role necessarily contributes towards the achievement of that end. Some supporters render their cause a disservice by overstating it or by advocating policies which, while in accordance with their own private financial interests, cannot be upheld on grounds of the public interest. For instance spokesmen of gold-producing interests in the United States do their best to spoil a good case by advocating a resumption of convertibility for the benefit of residents in the United States. Quite obviously no consideration of public interest calls for the dispersal of American monetary gold among private hoarders, whether within or outside the United States. Had domestic convertibility been resumed at the price of $35, or should it be resumed at the new price of $38, it would simply mean a free gift to speculators.

It would be difficult to find one single valid argument even in favour of a resumption of convertibility for non-resident hoarders and speculators. The Johnson Administration was very wise in stopping the dispersal of monetary gold stocks through the Central Banks' Gold Pool in 1968, and I sincerely hope that no Administration will ever be unwise enough to reverse that decision. As for converting dollars for the benefit of United States residents, it has been widely advocated for a great many years with great persistence and with an enthusiasm that was bordering on the fanatical. Economists and others who ought to have known better repeated to boredom in all seriousness their demand that the issue of American gold coins for domestic holders should be resumed. Even though the gold reserve was much larger at the time, it was almost a matter of simple arithmetic to predict how much time it would have taken for the official gold reserve to disappear in private hoards. Today the gold reserve is much smaller and the chances of a further rise of its price are much more obvious. Having regard to the fact that the free market price is well above the official American price, it would be offering a free gift to hoarders and

speculators to resume the issue of coins or to convert dollars
into gold bars.

Agitation in favour of such a measure tends to discredit the
case for a higher price of gold because many agitators are
prompted too obviously by their personal interests with a total
disregard of the public interest. Even after an increase in the
official price of gold to a level at which a further rise could not
reasonably be expected it would be advisable to retain the gold
stock for official purposes instead of distributing it among
private hoarders and speculators. It is always easier to disperse
a gold reserve than to reassemble it again when it is needed.

Sooner or later a situation is liable to arise in which the
United States Government and Congress will no longer be in
a position to resist forces making for a substantially higher
price of gold in terms of dollars. That situation has not yet
arisen up to the time of writing. In 1971 the official American
attitude was: Let other countries revalue their currencies instead of expecting us to devalue the dollar. The outcome of the
controversy was a feeble compromise – a realignment of parities
on 18 December 1971, under which the dollar price of gold was
raised slightly while the price of gold in terms of a number of
other currencies was lowered. Although the extent of the *de
facto* devaluation of the dollar on 18 December 1971 was moderate, it was important because it constituted the first step
departing from the official view, held with mulish obstinacy –
that the gold value of the dollar was unalterable. But, even
though it soon became obvious that the extent of the devaluation of the dollar was not sufficient, the Administration
reverted to its old attitude. Since the mini-devaluation evidently failed to solve the problem of the dollar, let other
countries solve it by increasing the extent of the revaluation of
their currencies.

Quite conceivably there might be another and yet another
agreed minor realignment of parties, but other Governments
became increasingly reluctant to revalue once more, having
regard to the fact that the situation of the dollar deteriorated
further after its devaluation, as a result of the inflationary

policy pursued by President Nixon. The gigantic Budgetary deficit and the American policy of cheap money in 1972, which drove many billions of dollars abroad for the sake of the higher interest rates that could be earned in London and elsewhere, stiffened the attitude of Western European Governments. Official American encouragement of the export of American capital caused considerable resentment.

By 1972 it became only too obvious that American direct investment abroad was gravely detrimental to the balance of payments of the United States not only on capital account but also on current account. For the American branch factories abroad were competing very effectively with the American factories in the United States and captured the latters' market both at home and abroad. The policy of encouraging direct investment abroad was regarded as evidence conclusively proving that the United States Government attached more importance to gaining control of industries abroad than to eliminating America's gigantic balance of payments deficit.

This resentment was probably largely responsible for the revival of the EEC's currency unification scheme early in 1972. Although that scheme had been under consideration in 1970–71 no further steps were taken about it after the suspension of the convertibility of the dollar on 15 August 1971. The European Governments were marking time, pending progress in the direction of the projected international currency reform. But in view of the unsatisfactory attitude of the United States Government the Western European Governments felt justified in proceeding with the consideration of their European currency scheme, on the assumption that Mr Connally's behaviour would delay progress with the broader project. If the establishment of a European monetary system should harm American interests responsibility for it will rest largely with short-sighted American politicians.

While European monetary integration is in the distant and uncertain future, the first step towards it might be soon achieved. The establishment of a narrower band between the exchange rates of the countries of the enlarged EEC is bound to harm the dollar, because its role as intervention currency will become curtailed. For that reason alone there is everything to be said against the change, having regard to the importance of maintaining the strength of the dollar. But the task of those of us who argue on such lines is not made any easier by the American attitude.

The resulting decline of dollar requirements of European Central Banks would make them even more reluctant to add to their dollar reserves by supporting the dollar against selling pressure. It might create a situation in which it would become inevitable to allow the dollar to float downward, or the United States Government might have to decide on another mini-devaluation. It would be much wiser to devalue the dollar to a sufficient extent to place it above suspicion.

But the United States is not likely to effect a major devaluation in cold blood, in the absence of some major crisis. That crisis might assume one of several forms. Inflation is liable to become escalated to a considerable extent, and the dollar might become once more overvalued. In fact, the rise in American wholesale prices after the termination of the freeze by 8 per cent in February wiped out the effect of the devaluation of 18 December 1971. The balance of payments is liable to deteriorate further, and the growing reluctance of other countries to absorb more dollars might result in a sharp depreciation of the dollar.

Another form of crisis which is liable to lead to a major devaluation would be a further aggravation of the American problem of unemployment. The deflationary effect of such a development would cause an increase in the number of insolvencies and quite conceivably official quarters in Washington might arrive at the conclusion that inflation would be a smaller evil. If they could be enabled to inflate by the allocation of substantial amounts of SDRs so much the better from their point of view. If the elaboration and application of the Barber Plan should take too much time the United States might resort to the solution of major devaluation before the advent of the much-awaited additional billions of SDRs.

Unfortunately the chances are that, instead of resorting to swift decisive action the American authorities will try to patch up the situation by repeated mini-devaluations over a period of years or by allowing the dollar to float downward. The result would be an aggravation of conditions, not only in the United States but in the entire free world. Uncertainty would tend to paralyse trade. The United States will be drifting from one crisis to another in a spirit of increasing demoralisation similar to the spirit that prevailed in France between the wars and again during the 'forties and the 'fifties until the advent of General de Gaulle in 1958.

It may take years before common sense could be made to prevail. Meanwhile things would go from bad to worse. Sooner or later mankind will stumble on the right solution, but not before it will learn the much-needed lesson at the cost of a series of crises. Gold is certain to emerge victorious from the chaos in which its de-monetisation will throw the world. Is it really necessary to pay such a high price for learning by bitter experience what could and should be a matter of common sense?

And will even the victory of gold be really worth winning if during its 'interregnum' monetary indiscipline should cause a disastrous deterioration of the environment? While the damage caused by financial crises and even by economic slumps is not irreparable – soon after the Second World War the standard of living rose well above the level it attained prior to the Wall Street slump of 1929 – it might be impossible to repair the damage caused by pollution and the exhaustion of irreplaceable raw materials caused by the escalation of growth during the years of advanced monetary permissiveness. Statesmen and economists ought to bear this in mind.

Postscript

As this book is about to go to press a wave of speculation has developed about the possibility of a package deal between the United States and the Soviet Union, under which the former might agree to a substantial increase of the official American price of gold. Should Congress refuse to authorise the granting of a big American loan to the U.S.S.R., conceivably an increase in the price of gold might be resorted to as an alternative way of financing American exports to the Soviet Union.

Mr Connally's departure from the U.S. Treasury is interpreted as an indication that President Nixon is no longer rigidly opposed to a realistic devaluation of the dollar and is no longer under the influence of the school of thought favouring a demonetisation of gold. Time alone will tell whether these assumptions are correct. But while even a few months ago a major increase in the price of gold could not be expected for years, now the possibility that it might be decided upon in a matter of months can no longer be ruled out altogether. Hence the rise in the market price.

If the price of gold should be raised as a concession to the Soviet Union then the right thing would be happening once more for the wrong reason. But if the Washington Administration should abandon its stubborn resistance to resorting to that solution it could claim to have made that concession for the sake of establishing friendlier relations with the Soviet Union in the interests of peaceful co-existence.

Index

South Africa, 74–5, 98
Soviet Union, 71, 14, 80, 91 *et seq.*,
   116–18
Sparta, 15
Special Drawing Rights (S.D.R.), 7–8,
   18, 30–1, 48, 53–4, 63, 65–9, 76, 94,
   103–7, 109–13, 117, 123
Stalin, 91
Standard of deferred payments
   function, 9
Standard of value function, 2, 9, 46,
   59, 102–3
State Bank of the U.S.S.R., 92
Sterling, *passim*
Sterling Area, 39–41
Sterling exchange standard, 39
Store of wealth function, 2, 9
Strakosch, Sir Henry, 43

Supply of gold, 6, 12–14, 26, 34, 36,
   38, 47, 53, 104–5
Support points, 12, 21
Sweden, 17, 37
Switzerland, 20, 46, 71

Trades Union Congress (T.U.C.), 61–2
Two-tier gold prices, 11, 74–7, 81–2

United States of America (U.S.A.),
   passim

Voltaire, 16

White, Harry Dexter, 48
Wilson, Harold, 14, 97

Yugoslav National Bank, 86